FAMILY ASSET PROTECTION

DIVORCE, FINANCE AND THE MEDIA

—————————— ● ——————————

Law Over Borders Comparative Guide 2023

Edited by Marcus Dearle, Miles Preston
& Johannes Gasser, Gasser Partner

GLOBAL LEGAL POST

Published in 2023 by:
Global City Media
86-90 Paul Street
London EC2A 4NE
United Kingdom
Telephone: +44 (0) 20 7193 5801
www.globalcitymedia.com
www.globallegalpost.com

Editors: Marcus Dearle & Johannes Gasser
Editorial Director: Mary Heaney
Commercial Director: Maria Sunderland
Editorial and Production Manager: Debbie Knowles
Associate Publisher: Claudia Tan
Digital: Elanganathapillai Sivakanthan
Digital Content: Marion Stobie

Printed in the UK by:
TJ Books
Trecerus Industrial Estate
Padstow
Cornwall
PL28 8RW
www.tjbooks.co.uk

ISBN: 978-0-9935776-8-0

INTRODUCTION

Marcus Dearle
Miles Preston

Johannes Gasser
Gasser Partner

It's 31 years since I co-compiled one of the world's first international family law guides — 'A Guide to Family Law in Europe' — as a member of the International Committee of what was then called the Solicitors' Family Law Association, now known as Resolution. The guide came with a foreword from the then President of the Family Division of England and Wales, Sir Stephen Brown. A few months ago I was pleased to see from the video shown at a law conference a copy of that guide perched on a shelf behind one of Sir Stephen's successors, Sir Andrew McFarlane, in his chambers at court.

Since the publication of that guide, a number of other excellent and well-respected international guides have been produced, extending the coverage to worldwide jurisdictions, but again on a very broad range of family law matters. However, I have been struck by the gap in the market for a guide specifically focussed on family asset protection issues in a divorce context – especially on trusts and pre- and postnuptial agreement issues, as these are the areas in which wealthy individuals and families need particular help and guidance on. I have also noticed a need to include coverage on media and transparency issues, including on whether the press can gain access to and/or report on what parties have hitherto usually assumed would be kept private and well away from the often critical gaze of the media. This guide is intended to fill that gap.

Marcus Dearle
Co-Editor and Contributor

I am delighted to have worked with Marcus Dearle on this new book and also to write the Liechtenstein and Austria chapters with Bernhard Motal. This is increasingly an important area of international law.

Johannes Gasser
Co-Editor and Contributor

AUSTRIA

Johannes Gasser & Bernhard Motal

Gasser Partner

INTRODUCTION

Even though Austria is a civil law country and therefore not familiar with the concept of trusts as it originated in common law jurisdictions, it nevertheless offers other effective ways for asset protection. Among the various corporate forms, the private foundation (*Privatstiftung*) is one of the most popular in this respect. In 1993, Austria adopted the Private Foundation Act (*Privatstiftungsgesetz*) and established the legal institute of the private foundation (*Privatstiftung*) into its domestic law, which was, to a considerable extent, modelled on the Liechtenstein foundation (*Stiftung*). The private foundation is a separate legal entity without shareholders, mainly used for asset protection and success planning purposes. Similar to a trust, a private foundation can be qualified and used as a will substitute and can be set up as a vehicle to protect assets that might otherwise be considered matrimonial assets.

The Private Foundation Act (*Privatstiftungsgesetz*) was created with the aim to attract foreign investors and to provide an asset protection and wealth planning vehicle to domestic HNWI. The private foundation has become a huge success since then. There are currently over 3,000 private foundations in Austria.

Not only its excellent and efficient legal system, but also its membership in the European Union make Austria an interesting place for asset protection. Therefore, the Country in the heart of Europe is an ideal jurisdiction in Europe to protect one's assets from family disputes, including divorce proceedings.

1. DIVORCE AND TRUSTS

Generally, Austrian law does not recognise the legal concept of trusts as it is known in common law jurisdictions, but it is familiar with the term 'trust'. Some legal provisions explicitly refer to trusts and sometimes even contain a definition of a trust, such as the law on the register of beneficial owners.

Austria has not ratified the Hague Trust Convention, which governs the recognition of trusts in the signatory states. However, following a 2017 European Court of Justice ruling (Panayi Trusts) which upheld the cross-border mobility of trusts and foundations, Austria must accept the legal influx of foreign trusts.

Therefore, a 'trust' structure that is established under Austrian law must be reinterpreted as an agreement recognized by the Austrian legal system. However, it is generally assumed that according to the provisions of the Austrian international private law, a foreign trust and its legal consequences are recognized in Austria insofar as the applicable foreign law recognizes the trust. This basically means that in this case the trustee is considered to be the formal owner of the trust property and that the rights and obligations resulting from the trust deed or the relevant law apply between the parties involved.

Also, due to the fundamental principle of freedom of contract applicable in Austria, the agreement of a so-called *Treuhand* (*fiducia*) is recognized as permissible. This is in principle a contractual agreement where the trustee becomes the legal owner of the trust assets transferred to them. However, this legal institution and its consequences differ from the trust known in common law jurisdictions.

When a divorce is filed in Austria, if there is no agreement between spouses regarding the financial consequences of their divorce, the court must assess the maintenance and determine the division of assets in accordance with the principles of § 66 *et seqq.* Marriage Act *(Ehegesetz)*.

In contrast to most other European countries, the statutory post-marital maintenance claim is based in particular on the degree of fault of the parties. However, income and assets of both the maintenance creditor and the maintenance debtor may also be relevant, especially for the amount of the claim. When determining the amount of income, the earnings from assets need to be considered, which may also include benefits from a (foreign) trust. In accordance with the so-called strain theory *(Anspannungsgrundsatz)*, possible benefits to which the beneficiary would be entitled but which they do not claim may also be taken into account. In addition, the assets may be attributed to the settlor if they have a corresponding influence, i.e. has not made the so-called asset sacrifice *(Vermögensopfer)*.

In the context of the division of marital property, it must be noted that according to § 82 (1) Marriage Act assets which a spouse has brought into the marriage, acquired by reason of death or which a third party has transferred to them via a donation *(Schenkung)* shall not be included in the assets to be divided (§ 82 (1) of the Marriage Act). Therefore, in many cases trusts may not be assessed in division proceedings. In order to prevent abuse, § 91 (1) Marriage Act provides protection against circumvention – if one spouse, without the consent of the other, has reduced the marital assets or the marital savings in a way that is contrary to the spouses' way of living during the marital partnership, at the earliest two years before the divorce, the value of what is missing shall be considered in the division.

However, in addition, it must be mentioned that since 2019 in Austria the EU Regulation on Matrimonial Property Regime 2011/03 and the EU Regulation 2011/04 on Property Regime in Registered Partnerships are directly applicable. These so-called European Matrimonial Property Regime Regulations *(Europäische Güterrechtsverordnungen)* regulate the respective applicable national matrimonial property regime, the place of jurisdiction for matrimonial property matters and the recognition of court decisions in matrimonial property matters issued in another member state of the European Union. Thus, on the basis of these regulations it may well be the case that an Austrian court must apply the matrimonial law of another member state of the European Union in the division of a marital or partnership property. This applicable law may then provide for division rules that deviate from the system of the Austrian Marriage Act.

If a divorce is filed in a foreign jurisdiction, the provisions of the Marriage Act outlined above will not apply. Due to the EU membership of Austria, court decisions that were issued in other member states of the European Union are – as a rule – to be recognized, and can generally be enforced in Austria. Furthermore, there are numerous bilateral agreements under international law, which means that court decisions from various other jurisdictions around the world are recognized and enforceable in Austria as well.

1.1 Financial disclosure

Where divorce proceedings are filed in Austria, spouses have an interest in the determination of mutual assets for the purposes of division proceedings and the assessment of maintenance. Although the law does not generally grant a right to information and accounting, such a right is provided by Article XLII Introductory

Act to the Code of Civil Procedure and the Jurisdiction Act (*Einführungsgesetz zur Zivilprozessordnung und der Jurisdiktionsnorm*) for civil procedures. The prerequisites are that the maintenance claim is justified on the merits, the person entitled to information could not, or only with considerable difficulty, make a specific payment claim, and the provision of information to remedy the situation is reasonable for the debtor. Confidentiality obligations, which the debtor has entered into contractually towards third parties (e.g. towards co-partners of his company), do not, in principle, restrict the duty to provide information. Since, from the perspective of execution law, this information disclosure is a so-called non-substitutable act (*unvertretbare Handlung*), i.e. one that cannot be performed by third parties, it can only be executed with fines or imprisonment. The Austrian Supreme Court grants such a right to information also in non-contentious proceedings and thus also in division proceedings.

Where divorce proceedings are filed in Austria, there are no specific statuary financial disclosure obligations of a trustee other from the spouse's general duties mentioned above. Unlike in the case of child maintenance, third parties are generally not obliged to provide information with regard to the assessment of post-marital maintenance between spouses.

However, if an Austrian court has to apply the law of a jurisdiction in which trusts are recognized, and which provides for corresponding disclosure obligations, these must be fulfilled by the parties. As always when foreign law is to be applied by an Austrian court, it must be ensured that the applicable foreign provisions do not contradict the Austrian *ordre public*.

As mentioned above, Austrian law does not impose any specific disclosure obligations on trustees, so that even if there are foreign divorce proceedings and Austrian law is applicable, only the general disclosure obligations under Article XLII Introductory Act to the Code of Civil Procedure and the Jurisdiction Act (*Einführungsgesetz zur Zivilprozessordnung und der Jurisdiktionsnorm*) are to be applied.

1.2 Financial orders

Since there is no such thing as an Austrian trust, where a spouse is the beneficiary of a 'trust deed' established under Austrian law, it needs to be converted into a valid agreement under Austrian law as it would have been concluded by *bona fide* and reasonable parties. Even though a reinterpretation into an Austrian private foundation would be the most obvious option, this will probably fail due to the formal requirements. Therefore, in many cases a *Treuhand* (*fiducia*) will have to be assumed as agreed upon. Depending on the specific agreement, the trust property could still be assigned to the settlor in terms of liability. As a result, neither the trustee's nor the beneficiary's creditors would be able to access the assets. However, the Austrian Supreme Court has not yet had the occasion to deal with such trust structures that were established under Austrian law. The same applies to decisions made by courts in foreign jurisdictions, if Austrian law must be applied.

If a trust were to be established under Austrian law, it would likely qualify as a fiduciary agreement, *in concreto* a *Treuhand* (*fiducia*). Although such a *Treuhand* (*fiducia*) is in principle merely a contractual agreement between the settlor and the trustee and the trustee therefore becomes the legal owner of the trust assets transferred to them, pursuant to the case law of the Austrian Supreme Court (and prevailing opinion in the literature) in the bankruptcy of the trustee the settlor is entitled to segregate the assets held by the trustee in favour of the settlor. This ultimately results in exclusion of the trust assets from the trustee's creditors' executive access. However, this does not apply in cases where there are grounds for suspicion of damage to creditors. Creditors of the beneficiary of a *Treuhand* (*fiducia*) may, however, under certain circumstances also assert their claims against trust assets, in any case if the beneficiary has a legal claim against trust assets and the creditors of the beneficiary have such claims transferred to them by way of compulsory attachment of claims (*Forderungspfändung*). However, if trust assets are situated abroad, the court(s) of the country in which the assets are located may have jurisdiction.

The same applies if the basis for the payment obligation is a divorce ruling recognized in Austria.

1.3 Enforcement

The Austrian (procedural) law does not provide for instruments like contempt of court orders. If a payment obligation is not met, it can be enforced in execution proceedings pursuant to the Code of Execution (*Exekutionsordnung*). This may result in the seizure and liquidation of assets, but not imprisonment of the obligated party. However, as mentioned above, the subject of disclosure obligations are so-called non-substitutable acts (*unvertretbare Handlungen*) which cannot be carried out by third parties and may therefore be executed with fines or even imprisonment.

2. PRENUPTIAL AND POSTNUPTIAL AGREEMENTS (PNAS)

Pursuant to § 97 Marriage Act, spouses may deviate from the consequences of division in the event of divorce provided by law and conclude an agreement prior to or during the marriage, which relates either to all or only parts of the assets. The subject of such agreements can be both the marital savings and the marital assets, but there are different formal requirements (see below). However, it must be noted that under certain circumstances (such as inequity or significant deterioration of living conditions), the court may order legal consequences deviating from such an agreement. Under Austrian law, agreements in proceedings for divorce are also permissible (cf. § 97 (5) Marriage Act). There are neither formal requirements for such an agreement nor can the court order deviating consequences. Nevertheless, the general limits of the principle of freedom of contract must always be considered.

If foreign parties agree on a PNA or domestic parties conclude a PNA under a foreign applicable law, Austrian courts will generally enforce and uphold such agreements, provided that there was a valid choice of foreign law and that there are no *ordre public* issues that would suggest the PNA, or parts thereof, to be disproportionate or discriminatory. In such cases, it can be assumed with a high degree of probability that the Austrian courts would not enforce such a PNA and would consider it null and void.

2.1 Procedural requirements

If a PNA governs the division of marital savings or the marital home, it must be notarized in order to be legally binding. On the other hand, if a PNA regulates the division of the remaining marital property, the written form is sufficient (cf. § 97 (1) Marriage Act).

2.2 Spouse's financial claims

Agreements modifying the division of the legal marital property division system are not limited to the election of a matrimonial property regime but, as outlined above, can be deviated by the court under certain circumstances.

2.3 Children's financial claims

Between the parents no contractual agreement may be made that is detrimental to the child. This would be deemed an inadmissible and ineffective so-called contract to the detriment of third parties (*Vertrag zulasten Dritter*). Nevertheless, parents going through a divorce could, for example, contractually agree to divide child support among themselves or to pay higher child support than provided for by the law. Under no circumstances, however, may the amount of child support be reduced in such an agreement. In simple terms, all provisions in such agreements that are to the detriment of the child are invalid.

3. THE MEDIA AND DIVORCE/FAMILY LAW PROCEEDINGS

Pursuant to § 140 Non-Contentious Matters Act (*Ausserstreitgesetz*), oral hearings in all non-contentious matrimonial and child-related matters are not public. Furthermore, the publication of certain circumstances of private and family life, the knowledge of which was obtained through the proceedings and in the secrecy of which there is a justified interest, is prohibited and may be subject to criminal sanctions. However, the court may, if no party objects, open the proceedings to the public, provided that no circumstances of private and family life are discussed and that this is compatible with the best interests of the represented person. Thus, the best interests of the child are always the centre of focus. In the case of contentious divorce proceedings, the hearing is not public either, pursuant to § 460 Code of Civil Procedure (*Zivilprozessordnung*).

Third parties who are not parties to the proceedings (members of the media) may only physically participate in oral hearings in matrimonial and child-related matters if the hearing is public, which, however, is only possible in exceptional cases pursuant to § 140 Non-Contentious Matters Act (*Ausserstreitgesetz*).

In principle, it is not possible for members of the media to gain access to or publish court documents. Pursuant to § 219 (2) Code of Civil Procedure, third parties may only gain access to court documents with the consent of the parties to the proceedings and, moreover, only insofar as this does not conflict with the overriding legitimate interests of another party or overriding public interests. In the absence of such consent, third parties may gain access to court documents only if a legal interest in the inspection of court documents is shown to be credible. Members of the media, however, have no legal interest in gaining access to court documents.

As mentioned above, oral proceedings in all matrimonial and child-related matters are not public and the public can only be allowed by court order within very narrow limits. However, even if an oral hearing should be made public in individual cases, cameras and recording devices are nevertheless not permitted, since Austrian civil procedural law prohibits the production of recordings during public hearings in general, i.e. not only in matrimonial and/or child-related matters.

3.1 Reporting restrictions

Austrian civil procedural law does not provide for a formal application to restrict reporting. However, such an application is unnecessary since, as described above, public presence at oral hearings in family law matters and the inspection of court documents by third parties is only possible if all parties to the proceedings give their respective consent.

Austrian civil procedural law does not provide for applications by the media for orders allowing them to report on proceeding issues or gain access to procedural documents.

AUTHOR BIOGRAPHIES

Johannes Gasser

Johannes Gasser is Senior Partner of GASSER PARTNER Attorneys at law, formerly Batliner Gasser, one of the leading law firms in Liechtenstein and a Chambers Global top tier firm, which was established in 1954. Johannes Gasser is ranked by Chambers Global as a "leading individual" in Liechtenstein. He is admitted to the Liechtenstein and Austrian Bar and specializes in advising UHNWI in setting up, administrating and challenging and defending Liechtenstein foundations and trusts in international litigation and arbitration. Johannes is a frequent speaker at the Liechtenstein University and University of Innsbruck (Austria) on foundation and trust law issues and legal expert witness in UK and other courts on Liechtenstein law. He is a member (Trust Estate Practitioner/TEP) of the Society of Trust and Estate Practitioners (STEP), an academician of The International Academy of Estate and Trust Law (IAETL) and an International Fellow of the American College of Trust and Estate Counsel (ACTEC).

Bernhard Motal

Bernhard Motal is a Counsel of GASSER PARTNER Attorneys at law. He is admitted to the Liechtenstein bar and also took the bar exam in Austria. Bernhard advises international clients and specialises in the areas of foundation and trust law, asset protection, estate planning and international private law. He regularly represents clients in domestic and international trust and foundation disputes (arbitration and litigation) and inheritance and divorce proceedings. He is author of numerous books and articles in renowned legal journals. In 2017, he won the prestigious Kathrein Privatbank Foundation Award in Austria with his doctoral thesis "Fundamental Questions of Liechtenstein Persons- and Corporate Law". Before joining Gasser Partner Attorneys at law in 2019, Bernhard worked in the corporate law department of a renowned Austrian law firm, as research and teaching assistant at the Department of Civil law at University of Vienna and as research Assistant at the Austrian Supreme Court, where he has acquired outstanding expertise in his fields of work.

BERMUDA

Craig MacIntyre & Jonathan Casey
Conyers Dill & Pearman

1. DIVORCE AND TRUSTS

The concept of trusts

As an offshore jurisdiction, the concept of trusts is not only well recognised but central to Bermuda's commercial appeal as an international financial centre. Bermuda trust law is based on English common law trusts and remains heavily influenced by English case law, however, the law has been enhanced in certain areas by local legislation. Significantly, like many offshore jurisdictions, Bermuda has enacted firewall legislation designed to ensure that any trust governed by Bermuda law will be insulated against rights and claims conferred by foreign law, including claims on divorce. These provisions have been strengthened significantly by the recently enacted Trusts (Special Provisions) Amendment 2020 (TSPA). The most significant provisions are as follows:

- section 9 provides that the Bermuda court shall have exclusive jurisdiction to adjudicate claims concerning the validity, construction, effects or administration of a Bermuda trust;
- section 10(3) excludes the application of foreign law to Bermuda trusts; and
- section 11 which prevents the enforcement or recognition of any foreign judgment in conflict with the firewall provisions.

The legislation is significant in the context of matrimonial proceedings as it precludes enforcement of any foreign orders which affect a Bermuda trust, whether directly or indirectly. It should be noted that the TSPA defines a Bermuda trust broadly as a trust with a "Bermuda connection" and does not require either the settlor or trustees to be resident in Bermuda. The legislation therefore confers jurisdiction to make orders with extraterritorial effect.

General approach to trusts on divorce

Bermuda's matrimonial law similarly derives from UK law and the primary legislation (the Matrimonial Causes Act 1974 (MCA)) mirrors UK legislation of the same name. Although later amendments to the UK legislation have not been fully adopted locally (save for the 2023 implementation of the Matrimonial Causes (Faultless Divorce) Amendment Act 2022), UK case law remains instructive particularly with regards to the approach to fairness and the pursuit of a clean break (notwithstanding the absence of a power to order a clean break in Bermuda).

The MCA provides jurisdiction to grant a decree of divorce and consequently make orders for financial relief provided the parties fulfil the statutory domicile or resident requirements set out in section 2 of the MCA. The court's powers may also be exercised following a foreign divorce provided that the divorce is recognised, although orders will be limited to interests and assets situated in Bermuda pursuant to section 9 of the Recognition of Divorces and Legal Separations Act 1977.

As in the UK, on any application for financial remedies, the court has a statutory duty to consider all financial resources which are, or are likely to be, available to each party in the foreseeable future, including those held in trust. Section 28 of the MCA provides the court with a broad discretionary power to vary nuptial settlements for the benefit of divorcing spouses. Alternatively, where the court is satisfied that distributions will continue to be made for the benefit of one spouse from a non-nuptial settlement, orders may be made against matrimonial property in the expectation that this will be offset by future trust distributions to the other spouse. It is possible for these orders to carry extraterritorial effect with regard to a trust governed by Bermuda law, thanks to the firewall provisions which confer exclusive jurisdiction of Bermuda trusts to the Bermuda court. However, where a trust is governed by the law of another jurisdiction, it is unlikely that the court would make orders as against either the trust or the trustees. Although the court's jurisdiction to make financial orders could be regarded as extending to trustees and/or trusts held offshore and governed by the law of another jurisdiction, in practice it is unlikely that these orders would be enforceable in the relevant jurisdiction and it is well-accepted that the court ought not to make orders that are incapable of enforcement. Therefore, in practice, financial orders tend to be limited in their reach to spouses, Bermuda trusts, and assets physically within the jurisdiction.

Divorce in a foreign jurisdiction
As a result of Bermuda's firewall provisions (see above) foreign orders purporting to vary a Bermuda trust on divorce will fall foul of the firewall provisions and will not be enforced by the local court. Spouses seeking to attack a Bermuda trust on divorce are therefore advised to seek specialist advice regarding the need to obtain orders directly from the Bermuda court.

Financial disclosure
All parties to divorce proceedings in Bermuda will be subject to a duty of full and frank disclosure and are required to provide disclosure of their assets worldwide, whether they are held legally or beneficially. This duty also extends to any resources which are, or are likely to be, available to a spouse, including trust assets.

Beneficiary spouses can be required to provide disclosure of any trust documents which are in their possession or which they are entitled to. A spouse cannot be compelled to provide trust documents which they have no entitlement to, however, they can be ordered to make a request for the same.

Parties are expected to provide disclosure voluntarily. Alternatively the court may order the parties to provide an affidavit of means, or specific disclosure to the extent that it considers this necessary and proportionate.

A spouse's failure to comply with the duty of full and frank disclosure may result in cost sanctions or, in extreme cases, a spouse may be held in contempt of court. Where a spouse's disclosure remains insufficient at trial, it is open to the court to make adverse inferences against them or make findings of financial misconduct and to reflect this in the final distribution of assets awarded.

Where the court is concerned with a Bermuda trust it will have jurisdiction to make and enforce orders for disclosure directly against trustees either by joining the trustees as parties, or, by making orders for third party disclosure.

In theory, the court may also make an *in personam* order against the trustee of a foreign trust to provide disclosure. However, given the practical difficulties arising on enforcement, the court is unlikely to do so in practice unless it is satisfied that the order will be recognised overseas or the trustee has submitted to the jurisdiction. In those circumstances, requests ought to be made to the trust's local court.

There is no obligation on trustees of a Bermuda trust to comply with foreign orders for disclosure made in contravention of the firewall provisions and enforcement by the court is similarly prohibited.

Financial orders
Proceedings in Bermuda
Domestic orders against spouse
It is permissible for the court to make orders against a spouse, in the expectation that further trust distributions will be forthcoming (commonly referred to as Thomas resource cases). However, in line with the UK case law in this area, such orders should only made where it would be reasonable to expect further advances based on previous conduct and care must be taken to avoid applying improper pressure on trustees.

The court will expect a spouse to comply with its orders, and will deploy enforcement mechanisms against those in breach of orders. However, the court cannot compel a trustee to exercise their discretion in a specific manner and enforcement mechanisms cannot be utilised against the trustees in the face of a spouses' refusal to comply.

Domestic orders against trusts/trustees
Provided the court is satisfied that it is dealing with a nuptial settlement, it has a broad power to vary the trust and may make orders against trustees or trust assets directly to facilitate this. Trustees will be expected to comply with such orders and will face enforcement proceedings in the event that they refuse to do so. As a result of Bermuda's firewall provisions conferring exclusive jurisdiction over Bermuda trusts, these orders may have extraterritorial effect, though in practice, consideration will need to be given to the issues which may arise on enforcement in a particular jurisdiction.

Foreign proceedings
By contrast, there are no obligations on either spouses or trustees to comply with orders made by foreign courts purporting to effect a Bermuda trust. The firewall provisions prevent the Bermuda court from giving effect to foreign judgments in breach of these provisions and compliance by Trustees would be a breach of their duties under domestic law.

Whilst the firewall provisions are yet to be tested in any reported matrimonial cases it was no doubt intended not only to prevent orders necessitating trust funds to be paid, but also orders which a spouse can only satisfy from their own funds if distributions are forthcoming to meet their own future needs thereafter.

Where orders against the assets of a Bermuda trust are likely to be necessary, these can and should be sought directly from the Bermuda court.

Enforcement

The court has a number of mechanisms at its disposal to enforce its own orders including an order for the examination of means, delivery of goods, possession and sale of property and garnishee proceedings. Deliberate refusal to comply with an order of the Bermuda court may give to rise to committal proceedings for contempt of court punishable by a fine or imprisonment. Committal proceedings are subject to the criminal standard of proof (beyond a reasonable doubt).

There is a limited statutory framework for the enforcement of orders originating from foreign courts. English judgments may be registered and enforced pursuant to The Judgments Reciprocal Enforcement Act 1958, provided the order does not stray beyond the jurisdiction of the UK court as recognised by Bermuda (which excludes orders in contravention of the firewall provisions). Maintenance orders are also capable of enforcement where orders emanate from signatories of the Maintenance Orders (Reciprocal Enforcement)(Designation) Order 1975.

Spouses seeking to enforce foreign orders that fall outside of the above framework will need to bring an action at common law for summary judgment.

2. PRENUPTIAL AND POSTNUPTIAL AGREEMENTS (PNAS)

Postnuptial agreements were found to be enforceable by the Privy Council (Bermuda's highest court) in *McLeod v. McLeod* [2008] UKPC 64. The court ruled that postnuptial agreements would be upheld unless there had been a change in circumstances or the agreement made inadequate provision for a child of the marriage. The decision in *Radmacher v. Granatino* [2010] UKSC 42 in which the UK Supreme Court held that prenuptial agreements would be given significant weight provided that they had been entered into freely and were found to be fair. Therefore, it is highly likely that prenuptial agreements will also be given significant weight in determining the division of assets on divorce in Bermuda in the future. Whilst decisions of the Supreme Court are not automatically binding in Bermuda, it is highly unlikely to be reversed by the Privy Council and likely to be regarded as highly persuasive.

It is important to note that neither prenuptial nor postnuptial agreements are strictly binding on the court and it remains impossible for the parties to oust the court's jurisdiction. However, provided the agreements are found to be fair, the court will respect the autonomy of the parties to regulate their financial affairs.

The Supreme Court and the UK Law Commission's Matrimonial Property, Needs and Agreements project (27 February 2014) provided helpful guidance on the conditions which would need to be met in order for an agreement to be upheld, which included the need for the parties to receive legal advice, provide full financial disclosure, and sign the agreement no less than 28 days before the wedding. There have been a number of reported cases where agreements have been upheld despite failing to strictly adhere to the *Radmacher* conditions in particular, with a shift away from the need for formal advice provided the terms of the agreement were understood and with some agreements being upheld despite failing to meet a party's needs. It is yet to be seen how rigorously these requirements will be enforced in Bermuda but is anticipated that the UK case law will be followed closely.

Spouse's financial claims

There is no matrimonial property regime in Bermuda. The court possesses broad discretionary powers to re-distribute property belonging to either party having had regard to their resources, including assets held in trust. It is therefore both possible and advisable for PNAs to address a spouse's financial claims comprehensively, having provided disclosure (at least in outline) of the assets and resources the court would have regard to, in order for a PNA to be regarded as fair by the court. Failure to do so may leave a PNA vulnerable to attack on the grounds of non-disclosure.

Children's financial claims

Financial claims relating to children may also be addressed in PNAs and are likely to be upheld by the court, provided the guidelines in *Radmacher* are observed. Nonetheless, the court will retain the power to make further orders, or vary any existing order, making financial provision for children even where a PNA has been upheld in the first instance, as it is not possible to terminate financial obligations towards a child, even by agreement.

3. THE MEDIA AND DIVORCE/FAMILY LAW PROCEEDINGS

Family law proceedings are generally heard in private and, to date, there has been seemingly little interest in applications for the media to attend or report on cases without anonymity.

In the event of a contested application on either issue, the court would need to undertake a balancing exercise between the right to privacy and the need for transparency. It should be noted that the Constitution makes express provision for the exclusion of the public (and by extension the media) from hearings in a range of circumstances including where attendance would prejudice the welfare of a child or parties' private lives.

Children proceedings

The Children Act 1998 explicitly prevents the attendance of non-parties at hearings without the leave of the court and whilst this provision is not replicated in other primary legislation governing cases concerning children (namely the Minors Act 1950 or the Matrimonial Causes Act 1973) proceedings pursuant to those Acts are usually held in chambers in any event.

The publication of any information relating to proceedings held *in camera* is prohibited where the court is mainly concerned with questions of a child's welfare, pursuant to section 10 of the Administration of Justice (Contempt of Court) 1979 Act. It is also an offence under the Children Act to publish any information, including the identity of other parties (such as Trustees), where this would have the effect of identifying a child involved those proceedings. As a result, there is a long-standing practice of anonymising judgments which primarily concern questions of a child's welfare.

Financial proceedings

Whilst there is no automatic bar on the identification of parties where the welfare of a child is not the main concern (e.g. where proceedings under the MCA concern financial remedies only), historically many judgments have been anonymised historically for privacy reasons nonetheless and, again, proceedings tend to be held in chambers.

AUTHOR BIOGRAPHIES

Craig MacIntyre
Craig is a Director in the private client and trust practice in the Bermuda office of Conyers Dill & Pearman. He joined Conyers in 1997. Craig's work encompasses a broad spectrum of trust, company, estate planning and asset protection opportunities.
www.conyers.com/people/view/craig-w-macintyre

Jonathan Casey
Jonathan Casey is an associate in the litigation department of the Bermuda office of Conyers. Jonathan is a specialist family law practitioner.
Jonathan specializes in all aspects of family law including divorce, financial disputes, and pre-nuptial agreements. He has significant experience in complex financial remedy proceedings, including disputes concerning significant wealth, and where there are issues over assets held within business structures or by trusts.
Jonathan also conducts proceedings in relation to children and represents parents who are often locked into fraught and highly contentious residence and child contact disputes.
In addition, Jonathan also conducts litigation between separating cohabitants in relation to property disputes, and separating parents in respect of financial claims.
Before joining Conyers, Jonathan practiced as an Attorney in the Cayman Islands and as a Solicitor in England.
www.conyers.com/people/view/jonathan-casey

ENGLAND & WALES

Marcus Dearle & Rahanna Choudhury
Miles Preston

INTRODUCTION

Divorce can impact on a trust where proceedings involve either the settlor of the trust and/or the trust's beneficiaries. Where trusts have been created, they will often hold a significant proportion of a family's wealth and the financially weaker party in a divorce commenced in England and Wales will often go to considerable lengths to ensure that trust assets are brought into account in determining the financial award from the court. Trustees face difficult considerations in this highly complex area and adverse consequences if they respond inappropriately — in *T v. T* (Joinder of Third Parties) [1996] 1 2 FLR 357 Wilson J (as he then was) ordered that the trustees should pay the wife's costs since they had tried and failed to set aside the order joining them as parties.

1. DIVORCE AND TRUSTS

Trusts have been a feature of common law jurisprudence for centuries and are fully recognised in England and Wales. The legal basis of trusts and the laws governing their operation are well established and understood. A trust is not, itself, a separate legal entity. It is, in essence, an arrangement whereby one person (the "settlor") gives away the enjoyment of assets to a group of individuals (the "beneficiaries", which will often include the settlor himself) while control of the assets and decisions on the administration and investment of those assets lies with others (the "trustees") who are bound by fiduciary duties in their dealings with both the assets and the beneficiaries. The principal terms by which the trustees manage the assets and allocate benefits to the beneficiaries are set out in the trust deed. The deed is approved by the settlor and, in most cases, is supplemented by a letter of wishes or memorandum of guidance. These ancillary documents are less formal than the trust deed itself but will typically outline the settlor's family's philosophy and will offer the trustees guidance on the long-term strategy the settlor has in mind for the assets settled on trust. A letter of wishes will typically be expressed to say that it does not purport to have legal effect nor to bind the trustees.

There are a number of different approaches that might be taken by the England and Wales family courts in relation to trusts — it makes no difference whether those trusts are based in England and Wales or offshore.

The basic approaches are to:
- Treat the trust as a financial resource. The court can make an order against a spouse with trust interests personally, and it is left to the spouse to work out how the liability will be met. This is on the basis that the trust is regarded by the court as a resource of the spouse, which may include a finding that in effect the spouse is likely to have access to the funds in the trust.
- Vary the trust if the trust is an ante-nuptial or post-nuptial settlement, for example, by making a provision for a spouse who is not already a beneficiary or removing a trustee.
- Treat the trust as a "sham" and that, in reality, it is a nominee relationship between the settlor and trustee.
- Set aside the disposition creating the trust.

The leading trust and resource case in England and Wales is *Charman v. Charman* [2005] EWCA Civ 1606, in which a 'likelihood test' in resource cases was first propounded. Wilson LJ at paragraph 13 stated that, "albeit with one small qualification, I agree with the suggestion of Butler-Sloss LJ in this court in *Browne v. Browne* [1989] 1 FLR 291, that, in this context, the question is more appropriately expressed as whether the spouse has 'immediate access to the funds' of the trust than 'effective control' over it. The qualification relates to the word 'immediate'... the question in that case was whether [the wife's] access to [the trust funds] was immediate. In principle, however, in the light of section 25(2)(a) of the 1973 Act, the question is surely whether the trustee would be likely to advance the capital immediately or in the foreseeable future".

A court can only exercise its jurisdiction to vary a trust if that trust is found to be nuptial. If a trust is found to be nuptial the England and Wales court has broad powers to vary it to the extent required properly and fairly to dispose of a spouse's financial claims. Variation tends to be a last resort and, typically, is only ordered if financial claims cannot be met with non-trust assets. In *Ben Hashem v. Al Shayif* [2009] 1 FLR 115, Moylan J (as he then was) stated: "[24] In addition, in the decision of *Ben Hashem v. Ali Shayif...* Munby J (as he then was), when summarising the matters which the court will take into account when dealing with applications for the variation of a settlement, included the following: "(iv) The settlement ought not to be interfered with further than is necessary to achieve that purpose, in other words to do justice between the parties; (v) Specifically, the court ought to be very slow to deprive innocent third parties of their rights under the settlement. If their interests are to be adversely affected then the court, looking at the wider picture, will normally seek to ensure that they receive some benefit which, even if not pecuniary, is approximately equivalent, so that they do not suffer substantial injury. As Sheldon J put it in the passage in Cartwright which I have already quoted: 'if and in so far as [the variation] would affect the interests of the child, it should be permitted only if, after taking into account all the terms of the intended order, all monetary considerations and any other relevant factors, however intangible, it can be said, on the whole, to be for their benefit or, at least, not to their disadvantage.'""

The English family court is clearly under an obligation to consider the interests of beneficiaries when deciding whether, and if so how, to exercise its powers to vary settlements: this is consistent with the wider approach referred to by the Court of Appeal in *Charman v. Charman* (No. 4) [2007] EWCA Civ 503 at paragraph 57: "it is essential for the court to bring to it a judicious mixture of worldly realism and of respect for the legal effects of trusts, the legal duties of trustees and, in the case of off-shore trusts, the jurisdiction of off-shore courts."

Following the leading English House of Lords decision in *Brooks v. Brooks* [1996] AC 375 a "nuptial settlement" is "one which makes some form of continuing provision for both OR either of the parties to a marriage, with or without provision for their children". So a very broad, and often widely interpreted, definition. In *Brooks* the court treated a private pension as a nuptial settlement.

N v. N [2006] EWHC 2908 (Fam) is an example of the innovative approach taken by the English Family Division in which a Bahamian law trust, which was not a nuptial settlement, had purchased the family home. Coleridge J said that his "task was to consider what the real substance of the arrangement was which governed this property". He held that the property itself was owned by a separate nuptial settlement capable of variation.

To determine whether a trust is a nuptial settlement, the first question is: is the trust "a settlement". If the answer is "yes", the second question is: is the settlement "nuptial" in character? This is a significantly fact- sensitive area. There is no real consistency in approach.

The financially weaker spouse will sometimes claim that the assets are, in reality, still owned by the settlor under a nominee or bare trust arrangement and the parties to the trust deed have not intended to create a trust but have intended, quite deliberately, to give a false impression to third parties and to the court. If the trust is a sham, then the application will be determined on the basis that the trust assets are still owned by the settlor. The trust will be invalid and ineffective. In practice, a finding of sham is rare.

Variation of settlement orders and set-aside orders are explored further below.

Financial disclosure

The financial disclosure obligations of a spouse in divorce proceedings filed in England and Wales relating to their trust interests on a worldwide basis are substantial and far-reaching. The spouse is required to provide full and frank disclosure in a detailed financial statement called a Form E (which must be signed with a statement of truth), together with full documentary evidence in support. It has a specific section dealing with trusts requiring details to be provided of any "Trust Interests (include interests under a discretionary trust), stating your estimate of the value of the interest and when it is likely to become realisable. If you say it will never be realisable or has no value, give your reasons".

That obligation is ongoing and requires the disclosure of all relevant documents whenever they come into the spouse's possession. A standard questionnaire seeking initial further information and documents regarding trust interests will ask for:

- a copy of the trust deed and all supplemental documents, for example deeds of appointment and deeds of variation;
- copies of the trust accounts for the last three available years;
- documentary evidence in the form of a schedule prepared or authenticated by one of the trustees of all capital advanced and income paid to the spouse from the trust since its creation, together with any loans made;
- an estimate of the income, and if applicable, capital advances which the spouse can reasonably expect to receive from the trust in the foreseeable future; and
- a copy of all letters of wishes and other documents stating the settlor's wishes.

Whether or not trustees are joined into divorce proceedings as a party, the England and Wales court will still expect trustees to co-operate and assist with the provision of disclosure whether the trust is an England and Wales trust or an offshore trust. The court is likely to join trustees into the proceedings in most cases where there are substantial assets held in trust.

In the event trustees are joined as a party to the proceedings, the court could order them to produce any documents which it considers necessary for disposing fairly of the attacking party's financial claims, or if so doing would save costs. In theory, this could apply to any trust related documentation which is in the possession, custody or power of the trustees. In these types of cases, typically, trustees are required to produce copies of documents including (but not limited to), trust deeds, letters of wishes, trust accounts, details of trust assets, details of previous distributions, details of previous requests for distributions or loans, details of previous loans, and (less often) correspondence with settlors and beneficiaries.

It is likely to be appropriate for the trustee to produce a succinct financial disclosure statement explaining evolution of the trust, providing an overview of the assets owned by the trust and explaining the fact that trustees are likely to need (a) to obtain the views of other beneficiaries who are not parties to the divorce proceedings and (b) then obtain the blessing of the offshore court in which the trust is based before giving any detailed financial disclosure.

There is currently some debate as to whether trustees should be joined as parties to proceedings when there is an application to vary trusts. In the case of *DR v. GR and others (financial remedy: variation of overseas trust)* [2013] EWHC 1196 (Fam), Mostyn J discharged the trustees as parties to the proceedings. He held that the joinder of trustees is not an essential pre-condition for the validity of a variation of settlement order as, once the trustees are served, the court can determine the matters in issue without the need for the trustees to be parties. His view was that if trustees are served with an application to vary, if they then chose to do nothing, any variation order would be binding on them (at least from the perspective of the English court).

In another English case *TM v. AH* [2016] EWHC 572 (Fam), however, Moor J took the opposite view and held that, in these circumstances, trustees should be joined to proceedings. The author considers Moor J's approach to be the more realistic one.

In some cases beneficiaries apply to the court to intervene in the proceedings. In that situation, as occurred in *Tchenguiz Imerman v. Imerman* [2013] EWHC 3627 (Fam), the court might well order the beneficiaries to disclose within the England and Wales proceedings documents and information from any proceedings that are being conducted in the jurisdiction where the trust is situated.

If other beneficiaries of a trust are joined, the court could order them to disclose within the England and Wales proceedings documents and information from the offshore proceedings. This is what happened in *Tchenguiz Imerman v. Imerman* (see above). In that case, adult beneficiaries of a number of offshore discretionary trusts were joined as parties on their application to intervene in the divorce proceedings. The court ordered the beneficiaries, as parties, to disclose copies of documents which had been provided to them for the purpose of an application which had been made in that case to the Royal Court of Jersey by the trustee of some of the trusts. The court made its order as it was satisfied that disclosure was necessary and proportionate in order to determine the substantive proceedings and that such evidence was unlikely to be forthcoming from any other source.

The court can order any third party residing in England and Wales to provide information and documents through an application to the court by way of a third party disclosure order.

The England and Wales court could issue a letter of request to the court where the trust is situated seeking information from the trustees.

The court might also make an order made for a Single Joint Expert to be appointed to investigate transfers into and out of trusts and provide a valuation of the trust assets.

In a case where divorce proceedings are filed outside England and Wales and there is an England and Wales trust, it is likely that the England and Wales court would require the trustees to answer a letter of request sent by the court of the foreign divorce jurisdiction.

The England and Wales court can draw adverse inferences if trustees fail to comply with an order. If a trust officer or director was visiting the jurisdiction of England and Wales, they could also be compelled to provide such disclosure by way of a third party disclosure order and could be committed to prison for failing to comply with a court order.

If the trustees submit to the jurisdiction, they would be likely to be expected to put forward a witness statement from a trust officer and to be tendered for cross-examination. Furthermore, if trustees submit this may engender expectations that they will comply with whatever order the England and Wales court makes, whereas the trustees would have to make clear this was not the case, which in turn could place the trustees in a conflicting position.

The court's reaction to trustees on disclosure issues will very much depend on how the trustees have conducted themselves. If the trustees will have already co-operated and given an initial statement providing some level of initial disclosure as explained above, the England and Wales court would be more likely to understand the trustee's situation and the fact that they may well still need to obtain the blessing of the offshore court in any event after a decision to provide financial disclosure has been handed down by the England and Wales court.

Financial orders

What types of orders can the court make at the conclusion of England and Wales divorce proceedings where there is either an England and Wales or an offshore trust?

- if the court is satisfied that a trust is likely to be a financial resource available to the spouse in the future, it could make a lump sum order against that spouse and/or the trustees (if the trustees are a party to the proceedings) pursuant to section 23 of the Matrimonial Causes Act 1973 (the MCA);
- an order pursuant to section 24(1)(c) of the MCA varying a trust as a nuptial settlement (see below);
- an order pursuant to section 37 of the MCA to set aside transfers into or out of a trust (see below);
- an order directing the settlor beneficiary to revoke a revocable trust (a Revocation Order (see below)); and
- ancillary orders or directions to effect/enforce a variation order and/or a Revocation Order.

An order pursuant to section 24(1)(c) of the MCA varying a trust as a nuptial settlement
Section 24(1)(c) allows a party to apply for, "An order varying for the benefit of the parties to the marriage and of the children of the family or either or any of them any ante-nuptial or postnuptial settlement... made on the parties to the marriage". The English court can only exercise this jurisdiction if a trust is found to be nuptial. In theory, the court's discretion to vary trusts is unfettered and can include (but is not limited to) ordering payments or transfers of assets out, adding/removing beneficiaries, adding/removing trustees, and the creation of sub-trusts.

An order pursuant to section 37 of the MCA to set aside transfers into or out of a trust
In order to exercise the power to set aside dispositions pursuant to section 37, the court has to be satisfied that three requirements are met:
- that a disposition has been made to a third party;
- that the disposition was made with the intention of defeating a claim for financial provision; and
- that if the disposition were set aside, financial provision or different financial provision would be made.

The disposition will not be set aside if the third party provided valuable consideration, acted in good faith and had no notice of any intention to defeat the claim. However, if the disposition was made within the previous three years, there is a rebuttable presumption that the disposition was made with the intention of defeating the claim.

Whilst the "intention to defeat" need not necessarily be a party's sole or dominant intention, the court is concerned under section 37 with the spouse's subjective intention: see *Kemmis v. Kemmis* [1988] 2 FLR 223, which was cited with approval by Anthony Chan J in *WYSL v. FHCBA* [2018] HKCU 2811. In *Kemmis*, "what had to be proved was not merely a dishonourable intention but a dishonest and fraudulent one, and the evidence which was required to tip the balance had to be correspondingly more convincing".

A Revocation Order
An order compelling a spouse who is also settlor and beneficiary can potentially be made to revoke any revocable trusts as a mandatory injunction, for example, as an aid to the enforcement of a lump sum. In other words, it could order the spouse settlor beneficiary to make a lump sum payment and direct him (either simultaneously, or more likely in default of payment, to revoke any revocable trusts). Should that spouse settlor beneficiary fail to comply with the court's direction, he would not only be in contempt and liable to imprisonment, but the court in England and Wales has the power to nominate a person in the settlor beneficiary's place to execute the necessary (revocation) documents. This is what occurred in the Hong Kong case of *H v. W* [2014] HKEC 955 (see the Hong Kong chapter).

Enforcement
The England and Wales court will want to do all it can to ensure that its order is enforced. In the event that the beneficiary has failed to comply with an order to

pay a lump sum, and the trustee has been joined into the proceedings, the court might well order the trustee to pay the lump sum. This could occur whether the trust is onshore or not.

In this context, it might conceivably seek to enforce the order by putting pressure on beneficiaries who are parties — particularly in the light of *H v. W* (see above).

The England and Wales court might also be persuaded (as a last resort) that it should make:

- a mandatory injunction in support of its order directing trustees to confirm their consent to the order (although the England and Wales court would not actually need their consent to make a variation order); or
- a prohibitory injunction preventing trustees from contesting the enforceability of the England and Wales court's order in the offshore jurisdiction.

A less draconian approach that a spouse might pursue is to argue that, having been joined to, and participated in the proceedings, beneficiaries are estopped from contesting any variation order in any courts both inside and outside England and Wales. Such an argument would not necessarily require any form of injunction from the England and Wales courts. The spouse could contend that the estoppel is an automatic legal consequence of the England and Wales proceedings.

In the event that trustees fail to comply with orders (for example for disclosure, payment of a lump sum, or for an order varying the terms of the trust), the claimant spouse may have to commence separate enforcement proceedings in the courts of the jurisdictions governing the trusts.

Although it is not a sanction as such, the England and Wales court can draw adverse inferences if the trustees fail to comply with an order.

If a trust officer or director of the trust were in the England and Wales jurisdiction, they could be compelled to comply and could be committed to prison for failing to do so.

If a party fails to provide financial disclosure and/or pay a lump sum, Judgment Summons proceedings could be taken out against that party resulting in them being committed to prison. An attacking party who secures a lump sum order and/or a variation of settlement order against assets situated outside the divorce jurisdiction might well find his success proves to be a pyrrhic victory because the order may not be enforced.

In the case of *Barclay v. Barclay* [2022] EWHC 2026 the judge Sir Jonathan Cohen, however, dismissed the substantive Judgment Summons brought by Lady Hiroko Barclay against her former husband, Sir Frederick Barclay, for non-payment of GBP 50 million (the first instalment of a total award of GBP 100 million). He stated "It might seem strange to an outsider that a court can find on a civil standard that a payer has the means to pay GBP 100 million and yet when he does not pay, finds that it cannot be satisfied to the criminal standard of proof that he has the means to make the payment... It will, however, be obvious that the arguments I have heard in this hearing are very different to those that I heard last year and an analysis of the differing legal concepts provides the explanation. My ruling does not in any way reduce H's liability to pay the sums ordered."

See also the Jersey chapter where it is stated that: "Recent Jersey authority — *Kea Investments Ltd v. Watson* [2021] JRC 009 — has confirmed that it is not possible for a judgment creditor, such as a spouse with an unsatisfied matrimonial award, to obtain execution against the interest of a discretionary beneficiary under a Jersey trust." In the Jersey judgment itself of [2021] JRC 009 in the Royal Court of 19 January 2021 the court held that: "Mr Watson is an adjudicated fraudster in and contemnor of the courts of England and Wales. Kea has the benefit of an English judgment including a declaration of entitlement to equitable compensation in a maximum sum of approximately GBP 43.5 million and interim payment orders of GBP 25,259,986.49, together with GBP 3,837,356.57 in costs.... The affidavits of... a partner of... Kea's English Solicitors show that despite considerable efforts at enforcement, a significant proportion of the Jersey judgment debt remains outstanding, and he deposes that there is a strong basis for saying that Mr Watson is engaged in an unlawful conspiracy with the Second Defendant ("Mr Gibson"), his "right hand man", to defeat his creditors, in particular Kea."

2. PRENUPTIAL AND POSTNUPTIAL AGREEMENTS (PNAS)

PNAs are not binding contracts under the law of England and Wales. They are however enforceable by the court and the court is likely to take them into account in a final award provided that the PNA is unvitiated and its terms are "fair".

In *WC v. HC* [2022] EWFC 22, Peel J succinctly set out the law on PNAs and stated: "22. I do not need to look beyond *Radmacher v. Granatino* [2010] UKSC 42 from which the following essential propositions can be drawn:

  i.   There is no material distinction between an ante-nuptial agreement and a postnuptial agreement (para 57).

  ii. If an ante-nuptial agreement, or indeed a post-nuptial agreement, is to carry full weight, "what is important is that each party should have all the information that is material to his or her decision, and that each party should intend that the agreement should govern the financial consequences of the marriage coming to an end" (para 69).

  iii. It is to be assumed that each party to a properly negotiated agreement is a grown up and able to look after himself or herself (para 51).

  iv. The first question will be whether any of the standard vitiating factors, duress, fraud or misrepresentation, is present. Even if the agreement does not have contractual force, those factors will negate any effect the agreement might otherwise have. But unconscionable conduct such as undue pressure (falling short of duress) will also be likely to eliminate the weight to be attached to the agreement, and other unworthy conduct, such as exploitation of a dominant position to secure an unfair advantage, would reduce or eliminate it (para 71). The court may take into account a party's emotional state, and what pressures he or she was under to agree. But that again cannot be considered in isolation from what would have happened had he or she not been under those pressures. (Para 72).

  v.   The court should give effect to a nuptial agreement that is freely entered into by each party with a full appreciation of its implications unless in the circumstances prevailing it would not be fair to hold the parties to their agreement. (para 75)."

Procedural requirements

There are no separate procedural requirements for a PNA to be enforceable on divorce: the court's jurisdiction cannot be ousted by the PNA and the court makes the final determination as to the extent to which it is enforced (if at all) and the parties will need (subject to circumstances where the case of Crossley applies — see below) to go through the standard and lengthy financial remedy procedure of exchange of financial disclosure in Forms E, attendance at a First Appointment and a Financial Dispute Resolution Appointment, and then to a trial if the case does not settle. To reduce the risk that a court will treat the PNA as vitiated and given no weight at all, both parties should have independent, specialist, legal advice, they should provide full financial disclosure to each other and the PNA should not be signed too close to the marriage date. It is good practice (but not a rule) that the PNA should be signed not less than 28 days before the marriage. The case of *Crossley v. Crossley* [2007] EWCA Civ 1491 provides a "short circuit" to normal ancillary relief procedure in a PNA case where there for example is a short, childless marriage and the parties are independently wealthy.

Spouse's financial claims

PNAs fully cover a spouse's full income and capital financial claims on divorce including claims against assets held in trusts. There is no matrimonial property regime in England and Wales.

Children's financial claims

PNAs in England and Wales do not usually incorporate arrangements for financial provision for children.

3. THE MEDIA AND DIVORCE/FAMILY LAW PROCEEDINGS

Parties involved in family law cases in England and Wales should be made aware before starting proceedings that members of the media will generally be able to attend court hearings dealing with financial and children issues. Under the current rules, however, the court controls what can be reported.

The rules are now changing with the announcement by Lieven J on 18 January 2023 of the introduction of a one-year pilot scheme in Leeds, Cardiff and Carlisle resulting from Sir Andrew McFarlane, President of the Family Division's, report on "Confidence and Confidentiality: Transparency in the Family Courts" of 28 October 2021. Sir Andrew stated in his report, "The present system in the Family Court whereby a journalist may attend any hearing but may not always report what they observe, is not sustainable. I have reached the conclusion that there needs to be a major shift in culture and process to increase the transparency in a number of respects. The conclusions that I have reached, following an extensive review, are published today. The review has focused upon the dual goals of enhancing public confidence in the Family Justice system, whilst at the same time maintaining the anonymity of those families and children who turn to it for protection. These twin principles of confidence and confidentiality are not, in my view, mutually exclusive and it is possible to achieve both goals. In addition to a range of ancillary proposals, my main conclusion is that the time has come for accredited media representatives to be able, not only to attend hearings, but to report publicly on what they see and hear. Any reporting must, however, be subject to very clear rules to maintain the anonymity of children and families, and to keep confidential intimate details of their private lives."

Set out below is the current law which applies to all courts in England and Wales excluding Leeds, Cardiff and Carlisle and the one-year pilot scheme which has been introduced in Leeds, Cardiff and Carlisle.

The current law

The principal element of the current statutory scheme is section 12 of the Administration of Justice Act 1960: This covers children and other cases – but not financial remedy proceedings. The combined effect of this section of the Act and the court rules is that accredited media representatives and legal bloggers are allowed to attend a private Family Court hearing as of right, but section 12 prevents the publication of information relating to proceedings if they concern children.

The court also restricts publication of confidential financial information disclosed in financial remedy proceedings pursuant to the powers and principles established in *Clibbery v. Allen* (No 2) [2002] EWCA Civ 45, *Lykiardopulo* [2010] EWCA Civ 1315 and *HRH Louis Xavier Marie Guillaume HRH Tessy Princess of Luxembourg & Anor* [2017] EWHC 3095 (Fam).

Accordingly, the Financial Remedy Courts now ordinarily control the release of information for publication, where this is sought, by an express order. This is usually dealt with by way of Reporting Restriction orders.

The one-year pilot scheme

A key proviso of the changes is that the anonymity of individual children will be preserved. In his report, Sir Andrew said, "in my view it is possible to maintain the privacy of those children, whilst at the same time operating a much more open justice system."

Journalists will be able to report on family court proceedings for the first time. Initially, court applications and child placement applications made within court proceedings will be open to reporting and, after a six-to-eight week period, private law children cases will also be reported on. Financial remedy applications will not form part of the reporting pilot. Reporting will be allowed only by accredited journalists and legal bloggers.

A new transparency order will define what can or cannot be reported. The transparency order will also allow documents to be released to the press including skeleton arguments/case outlines/position statements.

Under the current law, cameras and recording devices are not allowed into the court room. The same will apply under the one-year pilot scheme.

AUTHOR BIOGRAPHIES

Marcus Dearle

Marcus Dearle is a Partner at Miles Preston, Immediate Past Chair of the International Bar Association Family Law Committee, and a Fellow of the International Academy of Family Lawyers. He is a 26-year veteran of Withers in London and Hong Kong and has over 34 years of experience acting in complex domestic and international family law cases. Marcus has specialist expertise, in particular acting for trustees in HNW and UHNW divorce and trust cases, advising on UHNW pre- and post-nuptial agreements (PNAs) and dealing with international divorce litigation involving PNAs and trusts. He also has recognised pioneering expertise in international surrogacy law and medico-legal/fertility law issues. In addition to being admitted in England and Wales, he uniquely practises in Hong Kong family law from London. He is also admitted, but not practising in, the BVI. Marcus is recognised as a leading trusts and divorce litigation practitioner, advising UHNW clients in Legal Week's Private Client Global Elite directory: the directory is entirely reliant on peer nominations. He represented the trustee, HSBC International Limited, in the landmark Otto Poon Court of Final Appeal case and for the financially stronger husband in LCYP v JEK: both are Hong Kong cases. He currently represents Sir Frederick Barclay in his divorce - defending him in complex committal proceedings involving international trusts. He took over the case just after the family remedy trial judgment on 31 March 2021: see the reported judgments – Barclay v Barclay [2021] EWFC 40, 5 July 2021, and Barclay v Barclay [2022] EWHC 2026 (Fam), 28 July 2022.

Rahanna Choudhury

Rahanna is a 5-year qualified associate who has significant experience in all aspects of family law, with a particular focus on high net worth and ultra high net worth financial cases. Many of Rahanna's cases have an international element, such as dealing with complex asset structures, trusts and family businesses. Rahanna also has extensive experience of dealing with the most challenging aspects of private children's work, often involving safeguarding and welfare issues. She has particular experience of dealing with cases involving the appointment of guardians and allegations of domestic abuse. Rahanna joined Miles Preston in January 2023, having spent her time upon qualification at a leading regional boutique practice, under the mentorship of Claire Hamilton-Russell who was formerly a partner in the family law team at Farrer & Co. Rahanna is valued by her clients for giving clear, pragmatic advice at what is the most difficult of times. Rahanna is tenaciously committed to ensuring that her clients feel supported throughout the legal process and will always try to find a way to resolve matters outside of court if possible, if this is in her clients' best interests.

FRANCE

Charlotte Butruille-Cardew
CBBC Avocats

INTRODUCTION

French law and jurisprudence are becoming increasingly interconnected with other jurisdictions in Europe and further abroad. More than ever, judges and practitioners in France are encountering family asset protection concepts originating from common law jurisdictions such as trusts and prenuptial and postnuptial agreements. While these concepts enjoy a greater degree of recognition in France than previously, their conceptual underpinnings remain distinct from civil law notions. Accordingly, a number of questions remain unsettled. In this chapter, we consider how trusts are dealt with in France in the context of divorce proceedings, the extent to which prenuptial and postnuptial agreements are recognised, and the role of the media in domestic family law proceedings.

1. DIVORCE AND TRUSTS

Recognition of the trust in France

At its simplest, a trust is a legally binding arrangement which involves a settlor transferring legal ownership of their assets to at least one trustee, to be held for the benefit of at least one beneficiary.

Trusts can take different forms. In France, judges and practitioners typically deal with parties that may have interests or rights relating to offshore discretionary trusts or irrevocable trusts. For the purposes of French jurisprudence, a discretionary trust is a trust where the trustee has discretion to decide whether to appoint income or capital to the beneficiaries and, if so, which beneficiaries will receive a benefit and how much. An irrevocable trust is a fixed trust meaning its terms cannot be altered except in special circumstances.

As the trust is a construct born from common law jurisdictions, it involves a set of legal notions that are typically distinct from civil law systems. As such, civil law regimes do not generally encompass trust law, or at least the concept of a trust as it is has developed in common law countries. Accordingly, it is not possible for spouses to establish a trust under the French legal system. However, trusts established offshore are recognised by judges in France. The general position is that the legal implications of a trust may be recognised in France unless doing so would be incompatible with French public policy. In practice, this bar is a relatively low one and in most circumstances a family judge in France will recognise a discretionary, irrevocable trust as a distinct relationship with its own legal implications.

Financial disclosure

The disclosure obligations of spouses and trustees in French divorce proceedings

By way of background, in France, when a marriage ends, each spouse is allocated a portion of the assets accrued during the marriage according to the matrimonial regime of the couple. The matrimonial regime is a set of rules defining the spouses' rights and obligations in respect of their assets. On the divorce of the spouses, the matrimonial regime is "wound up". If the marriage is dissolved by divorce, along with the assets received pursuant to the matrimonial regime, one of the spouses may receive a compensatory benefit (*prestation compensatoire*) by order.

Against this background, the spouses are under an obligation to communicate all information and documents relevant to determining the rights and interests of the parties and to the liquidation of their matrimonial regime (see Article 259-3 of the French Civil Code (FCC)).

In respect of determining whether a *prestation compensatoire* is to be paid to one of the spouses, the parties are required to provide the judge with a declaration certifying on their honour the accuracy of their resources, income, assets and living conditions (Article 272 of the FCC). Practically speaking, this article binds the parties to the proceeding (i.e., the spouses) and does not extend to trustees of offshore trusts.

There is no set way in which spouses must abide by their disclosure obligations, unlike in other jurisdictions where the parties are required to complete questionnaires or to provide specific documents. Instead, it is up to the spouses to request from each other the documents or information which they believe to be relevant. While the French courts do not have powers to sanction inadequate disclosure, the judge may draw adverse conclusions against a party who has fallen short of their obligations.

While in theory these provisions should ensure against the use of a trust by a spouse to conceal assets from the court, there is always a risk of this happening, as is the case in other jurisdictions.

Financial orders
Financial orders in divorce proceedings and trust implications
Financial orders – prestation compensatoire
In the context of French divorce proceedings, the courts may order financial compensation in the form of a *prestation compensatoire*. The purpose of a *prestation compensatoire* is to compensate a spouse for the disparity in lifestyle arising from the breakdown of their marriage. The *prestation compensatoire* is usually ordered by the Court in the form of a capital payment made by way of a lump sum or a series of lump sums payable over a maximum of eight years.

The amount and form awarded as the *prestation compensatoire* is always subject to the judge's discretion. Article 271 of the FCC directs the judge to fix the award according to the needs of the spouse to whom it is paid and to the means of the other, taking into account the circumstances of the spouses at the time of divorce and in the foreseeable future. In exercising their discretion, the judge is to have regard to the following criteria:

- The duration of the marriage.
- The age and health of the spouses.
- The spouses' professional qualifications and occupation.
- The time spent, or to be spent, on educating the children, or favouring the spouse's career to the detriment of their own.
- The estimated or foreseeable assets of the spouses, both in capital and income, after liquidation of the matrimonial regime.
- The spouse's existing and foreseeable rights.
- Their respective situations as to retirement pensions.

This list is not definitive and there is no mandatory or automatic formula to determine the quantum of the award.

Consideration of the trust/trust assets when determining the prestation compensatoire
There is little case law relating to trusts in the family law context in France.

Accordingly, there is no clear answer to whether a French family judge ought to consider assets in a trust or a spouse's interest in a trust more broadly when determining the *prestation compensatoire*. The answer is likely to turn on the facts of each case, the level of disclosure that has been provided, as well as the court's general analysis of the factors set out in Article 271.

Recent decisions from the Court of Appeal in Paris dated 7 July 2015 and 24 May 2016 (No. 14/08780) shed some light on the issue. The case involved the divorce of a couple, Mr N and Mrs G. In this case the court considered that in determining the *prestation compensatoire* owing to Mrs G, trust assets in an offshore trust established by Mr N were to be taken into account.

The trust in question was a discretionary and irrevocable trust settled under the laws of the Island of Guernsey. While Mr N was not a trustee of the trust, he was the sole beneficiary. Mrs G asserted that the trust held assets of significant value which ought to be considered as part of Mr N's assets for the purposes of determining the *prestation compensatoire*. On the other hand, Mr N argued that the trust was created in connection to his retirement plan so that he could attain pension rights in the absence of a retirement contribution in England where he had worked for many years. Mr N highlighted the discretionary and irrevocable nature of the trust as well as its separate status under Guernsey law.

In its initial decision, the Court of Appeal ordered Mr N to produce a number of documents including the trust deed and a valuation of its asset. In its second decision, the Court of Appeal found that in accordance with local law and the trust deed:

- the assets in the trust did not belong to Mr N;
- Mr N was the sole beneficiary;
- the trustee was bound by its duty to act in the best interests of Mr N as the beneficiary; and
- the trustee enjoyed broad powers to use the trust fund or part of it to support Mr N and provide benefits to him as the sole beneficiary.

Against this background, the court found that while nothing could oblige the trustee to distribute the assets to Mr N, the primary objective of the trustee was the protection of Mr N's interests as the single beneficiary. Accordingly, the court found "the retirement rights of Mr N were guaranteed under optimized conditions" and on this basis took the trust assets into account in determining the quantum of the *prestation compensatoire* owing to Mrs G.

Practical takeaways

While noting that the obligations of spouse beneficiaries and trustees of offshore trusts in the context of divorce proceedings remain somewhat unclear under French law, the following principles can be drawn from the above:

- **Local law.** In the scenario whereby a spouse argues that trust assets or interests ought to be taken into account, the Court will likely analyse the trust in question closely, in accordance with the law under which it was established and is administered (see above and *Ziesennis* 20 February 1996, No. 93–19855).
- **Disclosure.** While the French courts may request the parties produce documents relating to a trust (No. 14/08780), these orders are not obligatory and there is no basis to support an order directing trustees of an offshore trust to provide documents to the court directly.

- **Piercing the veil.** The Approach of the Court of Appeal in No. 14/08780 suggests that trust assets may be taken into account, at least in some indirect way, by judges when determining the *protestation compensatoire* to be paid to a spouse in circumstances where the spouse is guaranteed to receive the trust asset or to benefit.

Enforcement

As we note above, the French family court judge does not enjoy powers to enforce the parties' disclosure obligations in the context of a divorce proceeding.

However, there are specific systems in place allowing for the enforcement of financial orders in family matters and specifically in respect of the non-payment of the *protestation compensatoire*. Typically, a bailiff will be engaged at the request of the spouse and may search the bank accounts of the debtor and/or seize their salaries and assets to prompt payment. The non-payment of the *protestation compensatoire* is also a criminal offence under articles 227-3 of the French Criminal Code.

Special procedures also empower the French courts to assist with the enforcement of maintenance orders from EU countries pursuant to the 2007 Hague Protocol. In summary, if the member state is also party to the Protocol recognition of the foreign maintenance order is automatic and the enforcement process can be commenced immediately. If the member state is not a party to the Protocol, or the maintenance order originates from a country outside the EU, additional steps apply.

2. PRENUPTIAL AND POSTNUPTIAL AGREEMENTS (PNAS)

In France, unlike in Anglo-Saxon jurisdictions, it is not possible for spouses to contractually organise all the financial consequences of their divorce in advance, alongside the administration and allocation of assets of the marriage.

However, spouses and future spouses in France are free to enter into a *contrat de mariage,* in which they agree on the matrimonial regime which they would like to apply during their marriage. As we have noted above, when the marriage terminates, the matrimonial regime of the couple is wound up and each spouse is allocated a portion of the assets accrued during the marriage based on the regime they have selected.

In order for a *contrat de mariage* to be substantively enforceable, its terms must conform with public policy. So long as this condition is satisfied, the parties can insert special clauses into the contract to suit their circumstances. In addition, separate formal requirements apply which we outline below. French marriage contracts are often recognised and enforced in other civil law jurisdictions and with respect to common law jurisdictions, often given weight by the Judge in their exercise of discretionary powers.

The provisions of PNAs drafted in accordance with foreign law will, under certain circumstances, be recognised in France. For instance, pursuant to the Matrimonial Property Regulation ((EU) 2016/1103), the French courts will recognise foreign agreements between spouses or future spouses in which the spouses or future spouses organise their matrimonial property regime. Generally speaking, in order to fall within the ambit of the Regulation, the agreement must satisfy formal requirements set by the Regulation (outlined below), comply with the laws of the relevant member states and be absent of any implications contrary to French public policy.

Procedural requirements
Domestic law

In order to be enforceable in accordance with domestic law, the form of a *contrat de mariage* must satisfy the following specific provisions:

- **FCC, Article 1394.** The contract must be drawn up by a notary in the presence of the parties.
- **FCC, Article 1395.** The contract must be concluded prior to the celebration of the marriage and shall take effect on the day of the marriage.
- **FCC, Article 76.** The spouses' marriage certificate must indicate whether a contract has been entered into and the name and address of the witnessing notary.

Spouses and future spouses may amend their *contrat de mariage* prior to their marriage, subject to the same formalities listed above. Further, parties may decide to change their matrimonial regime after their marriage however additional processes need to be followed.

EU law

In order to enforce a PNA under (EU) 2016/1103, aside from the substantive requirements stated above, the agreement must be in writing, dated and signed by both spouses.

Spouse's financial claims
Scope of agreements on divorce

As noted above, in France the recognised purpose of a *contrat de mariage*, or an equivalent foreign agreement, is to determine the matrimonial regime of the parties during their marriage. Bearing in mind that the matrimonial regime is the property of the parties held together or separately these agreements cannot provide for assets which may have been settled on a trust by either of the spouses as such assets are legally owned by the trustees and not the spouses.

In addition, a *contrat de mariage* or foreign equivalent cannot cover a *prestation compensatoire*, because this form of compensation is born from a disparity arising from the breakdown of the marriage. Accordingly, it is not possible for the parties to agree on a *prestation compensatoire* or to waive it ahead of time.

In instances where a foreign PNA caps a *prestation compensatoire*, the French courts will likely verify whether the amount is "sufficient" or otherwise contrary to public policy (see Cour de Cassation, 28 November 2006 (No. 04-11520) and 4 November 2009 (No. 08-20355)). In instances where a foreign agreement waives a *prestation compensatoire*, the French courts are not likely to recognise this part of the agreement on the grounds that doing so would be contrary to public policy.

Children's financial claims

By way of background, generally, when a couple separates in France, irrespective of whether they are married or not, the court makes an order with respect to parental responsibility, access (residency and contact) and child support.

In the case of divorce, the family judge will rule on each of these matters unless the divorce is by mutual consent. In this scenario, the spouses contractually agree to the divorce and all its consequences including parental responsibility, access and child support. This agreement can be set out in either a divorce agreement registered by a notary or in a parental agreement approved by the court. In all other circumstances, the court will determine parental responsibility, access and child support and the parties cannot seek to circumvent this process by way of a *contrat de mariage* or foreign equivalent as the scope of these agreement is in respect of the spouses' matrimonial regime only.

3. THE MEDIA AND DIVORCE/FAMILY LAW PROCEEDINGS

Reporting restrictions

Pursuant to article 248 of the FCC, hearings on the cause and consequences of a divorce, as well as provisional measures are not public. Accordingly, divorce proceedings in France are heard in private courts and the press do not have access to proceedings.

In respect of the judgement determining the outcome of a divorce proceeding, article 1082-1 of the French Civil Procedure provides that third parties may only have access to the part of the judgment that has been announced in public, that being the part outlining the findings of the court. This part of the judgement is usually introduced by the words "For these reasons" and, depending on the circumstances of the parties and their reason for divorce, varies greatly in length and detail. The names of the parties are redacted and replaced by their initials.

The rest of the judgment, as well as any annexures, may become publicly available after a period of 75 years from the date of the document, which may be extended to 100 years in some cases, or 25 years from the date of death of one of the former spouses, whichever timeframe is shorter.

AUTHOR BIOGRAPHY

Charlotte Butruille-Cardew
Charlotte is the partner and co-founder of CBBC law firm, Avocats Paris - France.

Charlotte has specialized for the last twenty years in complex high-net-worth cases, with an international element and involving tax and trust / foundation issues, substantial business assets and partnerships. She has also developed a particular expertise in international agreements (pre-nuptial, postnuptial, civil partnership). In addition, she advices regularly on patrimonial and assets structuring.

She is an accredited collaborative practitioner since 2006 and has developed over years an efficient expertise regarding difficult international negotiations. She is a Registered Foreign Lawyer in England & Wales.

HONG KONG

Marcus Dearle
Miles Preston

INTRODUCTION

It is has been firmly established in England and Wales and Hong Kong for many years that assets held in a discretionary trust are at risk of attack in divorce proceedings if either or both of the parties are beneficiaries of the trust. As reported court decisions in the court of England and Wales are regularly followed in Hong Kong and the law and procedure in connection with financial remedies cases in both jurisdictions is similar, the reader should read this chapter together with the England and Wales chapter: issues relating to submission to the jurisdiction, for example, are dealt with in more detail in the England and Wales and the law and procedure is essentially the same. One highly important area to focus on, however, where the law and procedure is both very different, is in the section on media issues.

1. DIVORCE AND TRUSTS

Trusts have been a feature of common law jurisprudence for centuries and are fully recognised in Hong Kong. The legal basis of trusts and the laws governing their operation are well established and understood. A trust is not, itself, a separate legal entity. It is, in essence, an arrangement whereby one person (the "settlor") gives away the enjoyment of assets to a group of individuals (the "beneficiaries", which will often include the settlor himself) while control of the assets and decisions on the administration and investment of those assets lies with others (the "trustees") who are bound by fiduciary duties in their dealings with both the assets and the beneficiaries. The principal terms by which the trustees manage the assets and allocate benefits to the beneficiaries are set out in the trust deed. The deed is approved by the settlor and, in most cases, is supplemented by a letter of wishes or memorandum of guidance. These ancillary documents are less formal than the trust deed itself but will typically outline the settlor's family's philosophy and will offer the trustees guidance on the long-term strategy which the settlor has in mind for the assets settled on trust. A letter of wishes will typically be expressed to say that it does not purport to have legal effect nor to bind the trustees.

There are a number of different approaches that might be taken by the Hong Kong family courts in relation to trusts — it makes no difference whether those trusts are based in Hong Kong or offshore — and these are broadly analogous to those that are available in the English courts, with many of the relevant authorities being English. English decisions are not binding on Hong Kong courts, but treated as highly persuasive authorities.

The basic approaches are to:

- treat the trust as a financial resource. The court can make an order against a spouse with trust interests personally, and it is left to the spouse to work out how the liability will be met. This is on the basis that the trust is regarded by the court as a resource of the spouse, which may include a finding that in effect the spouse is likely to have access to the funds in the trust (see the *Charman* likelihood test below);
- vary the trust if the trust is an ante-nuptial or post-nuptial settlement, for example, by making a provision for a spouse who is not already a beneficiary or removing a trustee;

- treat the trust as a "sham" and that in reality it is a nominee relationship between the settlor and trustee; and
- set aside the disposition creating the trust.

The leading trust and resource case in Hong Kong is *Kan Lai Kwan (KLK) v. Poon Lok To Otto & Anor* [2014] HKFLR 329 ("*Otto Poon*"). The case largely confirmed the English Court of Appeal's approach in the English case of *Charman v. Charman* (see England and Wales chapter).

The key conclusions drawn from *Otto Poon* are:

- The Court of Final Appeal clearly and unequivocally confirmed that the likelihood test in *Charman* is law in Hong Kong. In other words, the critical question will be "would the trustees be likely to advance all of the capital of the trust to the husband on his request?".
- The trust deeds standard term expressly authorising the trustee "to appoint capital and income to any one member of the class of eligible objects to the exclusion of others" was highly significant. In the event that neither of the parties (including the trustees) in the divorce fail to seek an answer to the likelihood test, the court will determine the answer. This effectively means that trustees will be expected to volunteer an answer to the likelihood test even if the question is not asked by any of the parties, including the husband and wife.
- The nature of the trust assets and the letter of wishes would also be significant. In particular, any reserved powers retained by a protector or settlor will be looked at very closely by the court.

A Hong Kong court can only exercise its jurisdiction to vary a trust if that trust is found to be nuptial. If a trust is found to be nuptial the Hong Kong court has broad powers to vary it to the extent required properly and fairly to dispose of a spouse's financial claims. Variation tends to be a last resort and, typically, is only ordered if financial claims cannot be met with non-trust assets. In the Hong Kong Court of First Instance (High Court) case of *H v. W* [2014] HKEC 955, the court cited *Ben Hashem v. Al Shayif* [2009] 1 FLR 115, and by way of overview stated: "the court's discretion to vary a nuptial settlement is unfettered and theoretically unlimited, but a settlement ought not be interfered with more than is necessary to do justice between the parties, and the court ought to be very slow to deprive innocent third parties (including children) of their rights under the settlement."

Following the leading English House of Lords decision in *Brooks v. Brooks* [1996] AC 375 a "nuptial settlement" is "one which makes some form of continuing provision for both OR either of the parties to a marriage, with or without provision for their children". So a very broad, and often widely interpreted, definition. In *Brooks* the court treated a private pension as a nuptial settlement.

To determine whether a trust is a nuptial settlement, the first question is: is the trust "a settlement". If the answer is "yes", the second question is: is the settlement "nuptial" in character? This is a significantly fact- sensitive area. There is no real consistency in approach.

1.1 Financial disclosure

The financial disclosure obligations of a spouse in divorce proceedings filed in Hong Kong relating to their trust interests on a worldwide basis are substantial and far-reaching. The spouse is required to provide full and frank disclosure in a detailed financial statement called a Form E (which must be sworn or affirmed on oath), together with full documentary evidence in support. It has a specific section dealing with trusts requiring details to be provided of any "Trust Interests (include interests under a discretionary trust), stating your estimate of the value of the interest and when it is likely to become realisable. If you say it will never be realisable or has no value, give your reasons".

That obligation is ongoing and requires the disclosure of all relevant documents whenever they come into the spouse's possession. A standard questionnaire seeking initial further information and documents regarding trust interests will ask for:

- a copy of the trust deed and all supplemental documents, for example deeds of appointment and deeds of variation;
- copies of the trust accounts for the last three available years;
- documentary evidence in the form of a schedule prepared or authenticated by one of the trustees of all capital advanced and income paid to the spouse from the trust since its creation, together with any loans made;
- an estimate of the income, and if applicable, capital advances which the spouse can reasonably expect to receive from the trust in the foreseeable future; and
- a copy of all letters of wishes and other documents stating the settlor's wishes.

Whether or not trustees are joined into divorce proceedings as a party, the Hong Kong court will still expect trustees to co-operate and assist with the provision of disclosure whether the trust is a Hong Kong trust or an offshore trust. The court is likely to join trustees into the proceedings in most cases where there are substantial assets held in trust. Once trustees are joined the court can make orders directly against them. The court could order trustees to produce any documents which it considers necessary for disposing fairly of the applicant spouse's financial claims. This could apply to any trust related documentation which is in the possession, custody or power of the trustees. In these types of cases, typically, trustees are required to produce copies of documents and provide information including the items listed above as well as details of previous distributions, details of previous requests for distributions or loans, details of previous loans, and (less often) correspondence with settlors and beneficiaries. If the trust is offshore, but there are trust officers of the trust situated in Hong Kong, then those trust officers could be subpoenaed to produce the documentation and information that has been ordered to be produced.

In some cases beneficiaries apply to the court to intervene in the proceedings. In that situation, as occurred in *Tchenguiz Imerman v. Imerman* [2013] EWHC 3627 (Fam), the court might well order the beneficiaries to disclose within the Hong Kong proceedings documents and information from any proceedings that are being conducted in the jurisdiction where the trust is situated.

The court can order any third party residing in Hong Kong to provide information and documents through a subpoena.

The Hong Kong court could issue a letter of request to the court where the trust is situated seeking information from the trustees.

The court might also make an order made for a Single Joint Expert to be appointed to investigate transfers into and out of trusts and provide a valuation of the trust assets.

If offshore trustees submit to the Hong Kong jurisdiction they would likely be expected to put forward a witness statement from a trust officer and to be tendered for cross-examination.

In a case where divorce proceedings are filed outside Hong Kong and there is a Hong Kong trust, the Hong Kong court would be likely to require the trustees to answer a letter of request sent by the court of the foreign divorce jurisdiction.

1.2 Financial orders

What types of orders can the court make at the conclusion of Hong Kong divorce proceedings where there is either a Hong Kong or an offshore trust?

- if the court is satisfied that a trust is likely to be a financial resource available to the spouse in the future, it could make a lump sum order against that spouse and/or the trustees (if the trustees are a party to the proceedings pursuant to section 4 of the Matrimonial Proceedings and Property Ordinance (MPPO);
- an order pursuant to section 6(1)(c) of MPPO varying a trust as a nuptial settlement (see below);
- an order pursuant to section 17(1)(b) of MPPO to set aside transfers into or out of a trust (see below);
- an order directing the settlor beneficiary to revoke a revocable trust (a Revocation Order (see below)); and
- ancillary orders or directions to effect/enforce a variation order and/or a Revocation Order.

An order pursuant to section 6(1)(c) of MPPO varying a trust as a nuptial settlement

Section 6(1)(c) allows a party to apply for, "An order varying for the benefit of the parties to the marriage and of the children of the family or either or any of them any ante-nuptial or postnuptial settlement... made on the parties to the marriage". The Hong Kong court can only exercise this jurisdiction if a trust is found to be nuptial. In theory, the court's discretion to vary trusts is unfettered and can include (but is not limited to) ordering payments or transfers of assets out, adding/removing beneficiaries, adding/removing trustees, and the creation of sub-trusts.

An order pursuant to section 17(1)(b) of MPPO to set aside transfers into or out of a trust

In order to exercise the power to set aside dispositions pursuant to section 17(1)(b), the court has to be satisfied that three requirements are met:

a) that a disposition has been made to a third party;
b) that the disposition was made with the intention of defeating a claim for financial provision; and
c) that if the disposition were set aside, financial provision or different financial provision would be made.

The disposition will not be set aside if the third party provided valuable consideration, acted in good faith and had no notice of any intention to defeat the claim. However, if the disposition was made within the previous three years, there is a rebuttable presumption that the disposition was made with the intention of defeating the claim.

Whilst the "intention to defeat" need not necessarily be a party's sole or dominant intention, the court is concerned under section 17 with the spouse's subjective intention: see *Kemmis v. Kemmis* [1988] 2 FLR 223, which was cited with approval by Anthony Chan J in *WYSL v. FHCBA* [2018] HKCU 2811. In *Kemmis*, "what had to be proved was not merely a dishonourable intention but a dishonest and fraudulent one, and the evidence which was required to tip the balance had to be correspondingly more convincing".

A Revocation Order

An order compelling a spouse who is also settlor and beneficiary can potentially be made to revoke any revocable trusts as a mandatory injunction for example as an aid to the enforcement of a lump sum. In other words, it could order the spouse settlor beneficiary to make a lump sum payment and direct him (either simultaneously, or more likely in default of payment, to revoke any revocable trusts). Should that spouse settlor beneficiary fail to comply with the court's direction, he would not only be in contempt and liable to imprisonment, but the Court of First Instance in Hong Kong has the power, pursuant to section 25A of the High Court Ordinance (Cap 4), to nominate a person in the settlor beneficiary's place to execute the necessary (revocation) documents.

This is what occurred in *H v. W* [2014] HKEC 955: the judge acknowledged in her judgment that the trustees had not submitted to the jurisdiction of the Hong Kong court and had been directed by the Cayman court not to submit. The judge stated, "The settlors and Trustee are required to submit to the exclusive jurisdiction of the courts of the Cayman Islands. In fact, in a judgment of the Cayman Court dated 24/12/2010, the Trustee was directed to refrain from submitting to the jurisdiction of Hong Kong."

She held: "the Trust be varied so that H be removed as a beneficiary of the Trust; any interests which H may have in the Trust (whether as beneficiary, settlor or otherwise) shall cease; and save as aforesaid, the Trust shall continue in accordance with the terms of the Deed, and with the 1st Respondent and the 3 Children of the family (namely, the eldest son, N and J) as beneficiaries therein and the 1st Respondent as sole Designated Beneficiary (as defined in the Deed)… The Petitioner do take all necessary steps and sign all necessary documents to facilitate and effect the variation of the Trust as set out in paragraph (1) above, and to divest himself of all interests, rights and powers under the Trust and the Deed (whether as beneficiary, settlor or otherwise), such steps shall include, but not limited to: sending the Trustees a written notice to the effect that the Petitioner relinquishes his status of a Designated Beneficiary pursuant to Clause 5(iii)(c) of the Deed; and giving written notice to the Trustee relinquishing and renouncing any and all his interests, rights and powers under the Trust and the Deed (whether as beneficiary, settlor or otherwise)."

Prohibition Orders

The Hong Kong court also has the power to make prohibition orders against parties in family proceedings who have failed to comply with financial orders by preventing them from leaving Hong Kong until the orders are complied with.

1.3 Enforcement

The Hong Kong court will want to do all it can to ensure that its order is enforced. In the event that the beneficiary has failed to comply with an order to pay a lump sum, and the trustee has been joined into the proceedings, the court might well order the trustee to pay the lump sum. This could occur whether the trust is onshore or not.

In this context, it might conceivably seek to enforce the order by putting pressure on beneficiaries who are parties — particularly in the light of *H v. W*.

The Hong Kong court might also be persuaded (as a last resort) that it should make:

- a mandatory injunction in support of its order directing trustees to confirm their consent to the order (although the Hong Kong court would not actually need their consent to make a variation order); or
- a prohibitory injunction preventing trustees from contesting the enforceability of the Hong Kong court's order in the offshore jurisdiction.

A less draconian approach that a spouse might pursue is to argue that, having been joined to, and participated in the proceedings, beneficiaries are estopped from contesting any variation order in any courts both inside and outside Hong Kong. Such an argument would not necessarily require any form of injunction from the Hong Kong courts. The spouse could contend that the estoppel is an automatic legal consequence of the Hong Kong proceedings.

In the event that trustees fail to comply with orders (for example for disclosure, payment of a lump sum, or for an order varying the terms of the trust), the claimant spouse may have to commence separate enforcement proceedings in the courts of the jurisdictions governing the trusts.

Although it is not a sanction as such, the Hong Kong court can draw adverse inferences if the trustees fail to comply with an order.

If a trust officer or director of the trust were in the Hong Kong jurisdiction, they could be compelled to comply and could be committed to prison for failing to do so.

If a party fails to provide financial disclosure and/or pay a lump sum, as in England and Wales, Judgment Summons proceedings could be taken out against that party resulting in them being committed to prison.

2. PRENUPTIAL AND POSTNUPTIAL AGREEMENTS (PNAS)

The leading cases on PNAs in Hong Kong are *SPH v. SA* (Forum and marital agreements) [2014] HKFLR 286 and *LCYP v. JEK* (Ancillary relief, section 17, prenuptial agreements & trusts) [2019] HKFLR 238; [2019] HKCFI 1588. In *SPH v. SA* the Court of Final Appeal held that the principles enunciated in the English Supreme Court case of *Radmacher v. Granatino* [2011] 1 AC 534 should be regarded as the law on marital agreements in Hong Kong.

In *LCYP v. JEK* the Court of First Instance (the High Court) considered whether the wife should be held to an unvitiated pre-nuptial agreement.

PNAs are not binding contracts under Hong Kong law. They are however enforceable by the court and the court is likely to do so provided that the PNA is unvitiated and its terms are "fair":

- An unvitiated PNA is one where there is no concern about the fairness of the circumstances surrounding the creation of the PNA: that there was no fraud, misrepresentation or undue pressure at that time, and that it was entered into "freely". In *LCYP v. JEK*, Mr Justice Anthony Chan described the word "unvitiated" as "a convenient label to describe a nuptial agreement which is not tainted by any vitiating factor, for example, lack of full disclosure of assets prior to the agreement".
- *LCYP v. JEK* has clarified the law on what is considered to be "fair" and provided guidance about the standard at which the financially weaker party's needs are to be assessed in the context of an unvitiated PNA. Anthony Chan J summarised, "in very simple terms where there exists an unvitiated nuptial agreement the application of which may conflict with the court's decision in its absence. The overriding consideration remains that of fairness. An unvitiated nuptial agreement is one of the circumstances to be considered in arriving at a fair distribution of assets. The court will have to assess its weight. In that assessment, needs and compensation would be important, whilst sharing less so."

2.1 Procedural requirements

There are no separate procedural requirements for a PNA to be enforceable on divorce: the court's jurisdiction cannot be ousted by the PNA and the court makes the final determination as to the extent to which it is enforced and the parties will need (subject to circumstances where the case of Crossley applies — see below) to go through the standard and lengthy ancillary relief procedure of exchange of financial disclosure in Forms E, attendance at a First Appointment and a Financial Dispute Resolution Appoint, and then to a trial if the case does not settle. To reduce the risk that a court will treat the PNA as vitiated and given no weight at all, both parties should have independent, specialist, legal advice, they should provide full financial disclosure to each other and the PNA should not be signed too close to the marriage date. It is good practice (but not a rule) that the PNA should be signed not less than 28 days before the marriage. The case of *Crossley v. Crossley* [2007] EWCA Civ 1491 provides a "short circuit" to normal ancillary relief procedure in a PNA case where there for example is a short, childless marriage and the parties are independently wealthy.

2.2 Spouse's financial claims

PNAs fully cover a spouse's full income and capital financial claims on divorce including claims against assets held in trusts. There is no matrimonial property regime in Hong Kong.

2.3 Children's financial claims

PNAs in Hong Kong do not usually incorporate arrangements for financial provision for children.

3. THE MEDIA AND DIVORCE/FAMILY LAW PROCEEDINGS

Unlike in England and Wales, the media are not allowed access to proceedings relating to finances and children in the lower courts in Hong Kong (that is up to and including the Court of First Instance — the High Court) as these proceedings are held in private. The media cannot attend hearings and are not allowed access to court documents. Cameras and recording devices are not allowed into the court room. In the very rare event that there is a contested divorce, the trial of the divorce will be heard in public.

3.1 Reporting restrictions

As all family law proceedings relating to finances and children are held in private in the lower courts, including up to the Court of First Instance (the High Court), there is no need to apply for any reporting restrictions orders in those courts. In the Court of Appeal and Court of Final Appeal, in cases involving minor children the judgments will be anonymised. In other family law cases in the Court of Appeal and Court of Final Appeal parties can be identified and this would open the possibility of parties making applications for orders restricting reporting.

AUTHOR BIOGRAPHY

Marcus Dearle

Marcus Dearle is a Partner at Miles Preston, Immediate Past Chair of the International Bar Association Family Law Committee, and a Fellow of the International Academy of Family Lawyers. He is a 26-year veteran of Withers in London and Hong Kong and has over 34 years of experience acting in complex domestic and international family law cases. Marcus has specialist expertise, in particular acting for trustees in HNW and UHNW divorce and trust cases, advising on UHNW pre- and post-nuptial agreements (PNAs) and dealing with international divorce litigation involving PNAs and trusts. He also has recognised pioneering expertise in international surrogacy law and medico-legal/fertility law issues. In addition to being admitted in England and Wales, he uniquely practises in Hong Kong family law from London. He is also admitted, but not practising in, the BVI. Marcus is recognised as a leading trusts and divorce litigation practitioner, advising UHNW clients in Legal Week's Private Client Global Elite directory: the directory is entirely reliant on peer nominations. He represented the trustee, HSBC International Limited, in the landmark Otto Poon Court of Final Appeal case and for the financially stronger husband in LCYP v JEK: both are Hong Kong cases. He currently represents Sir Frederick Barclay in his divorce - defending him in complex committal proceedings involving international trusts. He took over the case just after the family remedy trial judgment on 31 March 2021: see the reported judgments - Barclay v Barclay [2021] EWFC 40, 5 July 2021, and Barclay v Barclay [2022] EWHC 2026 (Fam), 28 July 2022.

ITALY

Raul-Angelo Papotti & Giovanni Cristofaro
Chiomenti

INTRODUCTION

The matter of family asset protection is growing in importance in Italy in a context where divorces are becoming more and more frequent and family events often take on transnational profiles.

Italian law traditionally struggled to recognise validity to family asset protection instruments since such activities have usually been deemed as fraudulent operations. However, as of today, and also thanks to the impulse in this direction provided by the decisions of the Italian courts, the use of asset protection instruments is recognized as a way of ensuring legitimate wealth preservation.

Therefore, despite the lack of Italian domestic legislation to trusts and the circumstance that prenuptial and postnuptial agreements are not provided for under Italian law, the use of the trust instrument is now widespread and continuous and there is some opening up of the courts with reference to the agreements that can be executed by the spouses.

1. DIVORCE AND TRUSTS

Italy did ratify the Hague Convention of 1 July 1985 on the law applicable to trusts and their recognition (hereinafter the "Convention") by Law 16 October 1989, no. 364, in force since 1 January 1992. However, as of today, Italy does not have a complete and organic internal regulation on trusts. Therefore, trusts set up in Italy have to be regulated by foreign governing laws, which must be laws proper to States that provide for trusts.

The foreign law which shall govern trusts must be selected by the settlor of the trust.

In light of the above, if compliant with the Convention and the relevant foreign governing law, trusts are recognized by Italian courts and enforceable in Italy, subject only to the overarching limitation of Italian public order principles; according to the consolidated Italian case law, "domestic trusts" (i.e. trusts in which the settlor, the beneficiaries and the trustee are Italian, the trust assets are located in Italy and the sole foreign element is the governing law) are also now fully recognized in Italy.

Such recognition will imply, in particular, that assets transferred to trust will be considered as a separate fund which is not part of settlor's/trustee's estate: it follows that trust assets cannot be affected by personal and property events which could involve the settlor or the trustee.

Despite the lack of Italian domestic legislation concerning trusts, the use of the trust instrument in Italy is now widespread and continuous. Therefore, Italian courts are increasingly faced with trusts even in the context of divorce proceedings.

In this perspective, in case there is a trust – compliant with the Convention and the relevant foreign governing law – that has been established by a spouse, who is thus the settlor of such trust, the Italian court will generally consider the assets part of the trust fund as separate assets that are not part of settlor's/spouse's estate.

It is understood, however, that in any case in which an Italian court declares the relevant trust as null and void for conflict with the Convention, the relevant foreign governing law or the Italian public order principles, the assets of the trust fund will be considered for all purposes to be owned by the spouse/settlor.

Conversely, in case one of the spouses turns out to be a beneficiary of a trust established by them or a third party, an Italian court could treat the trust and trust assets differently based on the characteristics of the beneficiary position and the nature of the beneficiary's interest in the trust.

Should the spouse/beneficiary of such a trust have an unconditional right to the trust's income or capital and do not have to meet any conditions for their interest to take effect (so called, "vested beneficiary"), the trust assets to which they are entitled could be considered part of the their estate.

By contrast, should the divorcing spouse have to meet certain conditions (such as surviving to a certain age, or surviving at the end of the trust) so that the trust assets can be transferred to them (so called "contingent beneficiary"), trust assets should not be taken into account by the Italian court for the purpose of determining the divorcing spouse's financial position, because the latter shall not be able to claim (before the trust's termination and/or before the relevant condition is fulfilled) any rights to the trust.

Moreover, it should be noted that trusts are increasingly being used by divorcing spouses directly in separation and divorce proceedings as a means of resolving disputes that have arisen about the headship and use of common property, with the aim also of ensuring the maintenance of children until they achieve economic independence. The establishment of trusts of this kind can be included in the record of consensual separation of the spouses, which is then subject to probate, or in the joint divorce action and confirmed in the subsequent court judgment.

Financial disclosure

Under Italian law, the spouses involved in divorce proceedings are subject to certain financial disclosure obligations in order to allow the courts to determine their financial positions.

In particular, the spouses are required to provide the courts with their personal income tax returns and any other documents relating to their income and property (both personal and common).

Accordingly, should one of the spouses be the settlor of a trust – which complies with the Convention and the foreign governing law – the latter should not be required to submit to the court any documents relating to the trust, since the trust assets should not be considered part of the settlor's/spouse's estate.

By contrast, should one of the spouses be a "vested beneficiary" of a trust established by them or a third party, such spouse could be required to comply with the mentioned financial disclosure obligations also in relation to their trust interests on a worldwide basis, since the right to receive trust assets could be deemed part of their personal estate.

In any event, please note that where case disputes arise with reference to the value of the spouses' assets and the court becomes aware of the existence of trusts involving the spouses in any manner, the court could be entitled to order the spouses to disclose any information about the assets transferred to trusts in which they are involved (the value of such assets also being able to be considered as an index of the spouse's financial position), and the spouses will have to comply with such order.

On the contrary, assuming the trustee of a trust is a third party – and not instead one of the divorcing spouses – there are no disclosure obligations imposed by Italian law burdening the trustee in the context of divorce proceedings filed in Italy. However, courts are given broad investigative powers also being entitled to order the trustees to disclose information about trusts and trust assets. Should instead such kind of requests to the trustee of a trust be made by one of the divorcing spouses, the provisions of the relevant deed of trust and/or the foreign governing law about trustee's disclosure obligations must be taken into account.

Moreover, it should be considered that Italy recognises trusts established in accordance with a foreign governing law but does not provide for a domestic regulation regarding trusts. Therefore, in any case in which trusts involving the spouses in any manner assume significance in the context of divorce proceedings filed in Italy, the existence of any disclosure obligations incumbent on the relevant trustees shall be evaluated, also taking into consideration the provisions included under the relevant deeds of trust and foreign governing laws. In any case, a clause which sought to restrict the court's right to make appropriate orders for procedural disclosure could be considered void as being an attempt to oust the jurisdiction of the court.

Financial orders

Should an Italian court order to a divorcing spouse, who is also a beneficiary of an existing trust, to pay a divorce award to the other spouse, the divorcing spouse/beneficiary will be required to pay such divorce award and they will be entitled to use any economic resources at their disposal for this purpose.

In the event that the spouse/beneficiary has no other economic resources that can be used to pay the divorce award imposed by the court and the court has determined that – in accordance with the provisions included under the relevant deed of trust and/or the foreign governing law – the spouse/beneficiary could obtain distributions from the trust, the latter will be obliged to obtain distributions from the trust in order to fulfil the payment obligations imposed by the court.

On the contrary, in the event that the spouse/beneficiary does not have other economic resources that can be used to pay the divorce award and does not even have the ability – in accordance with the provisions included under the relevant deed of trust and/or the foreign governing law – to obtain distributions from the trust, the court should not take their position as the trust's beneficiary into consideration for the purpose of determining whether they will be able to pay the divorce award.

Should an Italian court order to a divorcing spouse, who is also a trustee of a trust, to pay a divorce award to the other spouse, the divorcing spouse/trustee will not be entitled to use the income and/or capital held in trust for this purpose, since trust assets should not be considered part of the trustee's/spouse's estate.

Should an Italian court order to a spouse, who is also a beneficiary of a trust, to pay a divorce award to the other spouse and to obtain – in accordance with the provisions of the relevant deed of trust and/or the foreign governing law – distributions (or specific assets) from the trust for this purpose, the trustee of such trust shall be required to execute such distributions in accordance with the relevant provisions of the trust deed and the law governing the trust.

Enforcement

Notwithstanding the above, when trusts involving the spouses in any manner assume significance in the context of divorce proceedings filed in Italy, the failure in complying with any disclosure obligations issued by an Italian court incumbent on settlors, beneficiaries and trustees could be punished under Italian Criminal Code (ICC).

Several offences could be envisaged and, among others, the following could be taken into consideration:

- Article 483 ICC, ideological misrepresentation committed by the private party in a public deed; and
- Article 495 ICC, false attestation or statement to a public official about identity or personal qualities.

With reference to the above offences it should be noted that a person may be punished with imprisonment from 1 to 6 years.

Furthermore, failure to comply with capital and income payment orders may be sanctioned by Article 570-*bis* ICC, which punishes the conduct of the spouse who breaches the obligation to pay any kind of cheque due in the event of divorce or violates economic obligations in the matter of separation of spouses and shared custody of children.

Depending on the concrete circumstances, the judicial authority could order the preventive seizure of the not-disclosed trust assets.

Failure to comply with a disclosure order issued by the foreign authority is not relevant under Italian law, however the foreign authority may activate institutional channels in order to carry out certain investigations on trust assets.

2. PRENUPTIAL AND POSTNUPTIAL AGREEMENTS (PNAS)

PNAs are not provided for under Italian law. The only agreement allowed between spouses is a covenant by which they agree to change their matrimonial property regime from joint ownership to separation of property, or *vice versa*, without any reference to spousal support in the event of separation, divorce, dissolution, or marriage.

The Italian Civil Code does not mention the matter of spousal support among the subjects that a marriage agreement can deal with.

Therefore, from an Italian law perspective, PNAs would be considered null and void on public policy grounds, since they could impair the freedom of both parties to decide whether to dissolve their marriage or not: the parties' legal married status — which is a personal legal status — is not negotiable.

However, recently, Italian courts are gradually changing their view on the matter and they have come to recognize agreements by which spouses agree:

- that, in case of divorce, a property will be transferred, as compensation, to the spouse who has paid the refurbishment costs of a property owned by the transferring spouse; and
- that only one of them is liable for the repayment of a loan in case of a future divorce.

In that perspective, it should be pointed out that in December 2018 a bill of law was brought before the Italian Parliament that would allow spouses to regulate

— through PNAs — their personal and economic relationships, to prepare for any future crisis between them and to predetermine guidelines for the education of their children.

Without prejudice to the above, foreign PNAs are instead recognized in Italy if they are valid under the foreign law governing the property relationships between spouses.

Please note that, pursuant to Articles 29 and 30 of Law No. 218 of 31 May 1995 (the Italian private international law), the matrimonial property regime of the spouses shall be governed by their common national law (if any) or by the law of the State where their married life is mainly located; however, the spouses may agree that their matrimonial property regime shall be governed by the national law of one of them, or the law of the State where one of them resides.

Procedural requirements
With reference to specific procedural requirements for a PNA to be enforceable on divorce in Italy, no relevant provisions are included under Italian law since — as further explained above — Italian PNAs are deemed null and void for violation of public order rules. However, should the spouses have entered into a PNA pursuant to a foreign law which is recognized in Italy, the PNA shall be subject to the procedural requirements of the relevant foreign law for it to be enforceable on divorce.

Spouse's financial claims
Likewise, with reference to the possibility for a PNA to fully cover a spouse's financial claims on divorce (including claims against assets held in trusts) or deal with financial claims regarding children, no relevant provisions are included under Italian law since — again, as explained above — Italian PNAs are deemed null and void for violation of public order rules. However, should the spouses have entered into a PNA pursuant to a foreign law which is recognized in Italy, the PNA can have the content allowed by relevant foreign law.

Children's financial claims
Notwithstanding the fact that PNAs are null and void under Italian law, please note that Italian courts do, however, admit agreements concluded by the spouses, in the context of consensual separation or divorce proceedings, by which they regulate their personal and economic relationships arising from separation/divorce, including financial claims and guidelines for the maintenance of children until they achieve economic independence.

3. THE MEDIA AND DIVORCE/FAMILY LAW PROCEEDINGS
According to article 128 of the Italian Civil Procedure Code, discussion hearings must be held publicly under penalty of invalidity.

However, such general rule is waived by other provisions: for instance, access to public is not consented — pursuant to article 84 of the Implementing Provisions to the Civil Procedure Code — during hearings dedicated to collection and admission of proofs and evidences. Moreover, after the civil procedure reform of 1990, the "final discussion" hearing is no longer a mandatory step of the proceeding, so it is usual that an entire civil proceeding might take place without any public hearing to attend.

With specific regard to family law cases, since the COVID-19 pandemic, divorce and separation proceedings on mutual consent are all celebrated by remote audio-visual connection without the presence of the parties (subject to the parties' written waiver of appearance). This practice has remained in force to this day. On the contrary, divorce and separation litigation proceedings (i.e., celebrated without mutual consent) are still held with the presence of parties and their appointed attorneys: however, it is widespread usage for the court in all cases to order the hearing to be held *in camera* and without the presence of the public.

It should also be noted that, according to Article 76 of the Implementing Provisions to the Civil Procedure Code, access to case documents is granted only to defence attorneys, parties and judges, whilst the public does not have the opportunity to obtain them. Moreover, in case of particularly sensitive proceedings for which it is appropriate to maintain the confidentiality of the information (also with regard to possible interference by the press), the parties are entitled to request the court that the documents and records of the proceedings be kept in a strongbox or other duly supervised place.

Likewise, it is a long-standing practice that appointed attorneys, in order to have access to the files of proceedings concerning the minor-aged, must submit a special application allowing them to inspect the relating files for a very limited time in order to avoid the risk of disclosure of sensitive information.

Furthermore, the rules governing publicity of the hearings meets certain boundaries even in an international context, as the ones set forth in Article 6 of ECHR and Article 14 of the International Covenant on Civil and Political Rights of 1966. This rule provides that press and public may be excluded from all or part of the trial in the interests of morals, public order or national security in a democratic society, where the interests of those who are under-aged, or the protection of the private life of the parties, so require. The aforesaid provisions also establish that any verdict pronounced in a civil or criminal trial shall be made public, unless the interest of minors requires otherwise, or the trial concerns matrimonial disputes or the custody of children.

Reporting restrictions

On October 1990, the Order of Journalists, the National Federation of the Italian Press, and Telefono Azzurro — a major Italian non-profit organization established in 1987 with the aim of defending under-age rights — entered into the Treviso Chart, which is a protocol with the intent of regulating the relationship between information and minors. The Chart, on the one hand protects the right to report news, and on the other hand clarifies the power that all media have in building a society that fully respects the image of children and adolescents. The main mission enshrined in the Chart consists of defending the identity, personality, and rights of minors who are victims or perpetrators of crimes, or otherwise involved in situations that could impair their harmonious psychological development. The same guarantees are also provided to those who are marginal in society.

The Chart has set some binding rules of self-regulation for Italian journalists and, more broadly, for all news workers: among others, it is established reporters are required to ensure the anonymity of minors involved in judicial and news events potentially damaging to their personalities; journalists must avoid publishing anything that could lead to the identification of a child involved in legal proceedings, whether it is data (parental details, home address, school, etc.) or a photograph or film; in cases of separation or divorce regarding parents with minor children, adoptions or foster care, the journalist is required not to emphasize or make spectacular the depiction of the facts. In addition, the anonymity of the minors involved in these cases shall be granted as well.

AUTHOR BIOGRAPHIES

Raul-Angelo Papotti

Raul-Angelo Papotti is Head of Chiomenti Tax practice and co-head of Advisory department. Raul-Angelo advises on all areas of tax law, with particular emphasis on international tax law. He has a special expertise in the taxation of trusts and tax planning structures, and in estate planning, advising corporate and private clients alike. Clients include investment banks, private banks, corporates as well as high net worth individuals, families and family offices.

He is author of many publications on international tax and estate planning matters and is a frequent speaker at the most prestigious domestic and international congresses.

Raul-Angelo is ranked as a leading expert in the foremost international legal guides such as Chambers, Legal 500 and Who's Who Legal.

Giovanni Cristofaro

Giovanni Cristofaro advises Italian and international clients on matters concerning planning, management and use of family assets (including company shareholdings and artworks) with a focus on family wealth planning, including succession, intra-family wealth transfers and trusts. Head of Chiomenti Private Clients group since 2015.

He joined Chiomenti in 2006; he was a Firm Consultant from 2015 to 2016 and became a partner in 2017.

He is member of the Rome Bar (Italy) and Member of the Board of Directors of STEP (Society of Trust and Estate Practitioners) Italy.

Giovanni is ranked as a leading expert in the foremost international legal guides.

JERSEY

James Sheedy & Simon Thomas
Baker & Partners

INTRODUCTION

The Bailiwick of Jersey is one of the three Crown Dependencies of the British Crown that surround the United Kingdom. It is located in the English Channel, sixteen miles west of the French Normandy coast. It is not part of the United Kingdom's territory and has never been absorbed into the common law legal system of England and Wales, having been a self-governing territory for over 800 years, enjoying virtual total autonomy over its own taxation, legal system and domestic affairs.

Jersey's legal system has its roots in Norman customary law but has also been influenced in varying degrees over the centuries by English law and French law. Jersey's law of trusts is governed principally by the Trusts (Jersey) Law 1984, as amended. Its matrimonial law is governed by the Matrimonial Causes (Jersey) Law 1949. In the absence of local legal authority or legislative provision, Jersey will often look to judgments of English and Commonwealth courts as being persuasive (*Re Malabry Invs Ltd* 1982 JJ 117). Local legislation is enacted by Jersey's parliament, the States Assembly. Assent to local statutory law is effected through the Privy Council in London.

Jersey is not a part of European Union and is not subject to EU law. Therefore, EU Regulations concerning jurisdiction and the recognition and enforcement of judgments in civil or matrimonial matters.

The family court (the Family Division of the Royal Court of Jersey) has jurisdiction in relation to divorce, nullity and judicial separation (Matrimonial Causes (Jersey) Law 1949, Articles 3 and 6) where:

- the parties are domiciled in Jersey when proceedings are commenced;
- either of the parties was habitually resident in Jersey for the year immediately preceding the date proceedings are started.

The same jurisdiction rules apply for both mixed and same sex spouses and civil partners.

Financial remedies are generally applied for within divorce proceedings. Claims can be made for:

- Periodical payments (for children and spouses).
- Lump sum payments (with security as necessary).
- Property transfers.
- Orders for sale of property.
- Variation of nuptial settlements.
- Interim orders.

The Royal Court does not currently have jurisdiction to make a pension sharing order in matrimonial proceedings although, in practice, that is often compensated for by making provision from elsewhere in the matrimonial 'pot'.

1. DIVORCE AND TRUSTS

Jersey is one of the foremost offshore jurisdictions in the world for private wealth structuring using trusts. Jersey law recognises trusts whether governed by Jersey law or trusts established and governed by laws other than Jersey law. Jersey is a party to the Hague Trusts Convention.

It has a very well-developed case law concerning trusts and trust disputes and Jersey's principal court, the Royal Court of Jersey, and the Jersey Court of Appeal are recognised internationally as a pre-eminent source of leading modern trust jurisprudence.

A common issue in play in matrimonial proceedings involving Jersey is whether any resulting matrimonial award can be enforced against a trust in Jersey. Jersey has enacted legislation in Article 9 Trusts (Jersey) Law 1984, (known as the 'firewall') specifically to protect Jersey trusts from by interference of orders of foreign courts.

Where there is matrimonial claim to: i) vary a Jersey trust; ii) claim trust assets as part of a matrimonial award; or iii) treat a trust as belonging to a spouse or otherwise being a 'financial resource' from which maintenance or a lump sum is to be satisfied, the treatment of the trust assets could be subject to a range of analyses:

- Whether the trust is a nuptial settlement that is capable of being varied or subject to a property adjustment order under the jurisdiction of the matrimonial court (e.g. under section 24(1)(c) Matrimonial Causes Act 1974). This involves affirming the existence of a genuine trust. Where the trust is governed by Jersey law, and variation is sought as a remedy, early and careful consideration will be required as to whether any order made by a foreign court is capable of enforcement within Jersey. Where potential enforcement will be against a Jersey trust, the firewall legislation in Article 9 Trusts (Jersey) Law 1984 will be engaged.
- Consideration (particularly if the matrimonial proceedings are outside Jersey and the trust assets within the jurisdiction of the matrimonial court) will often be given to whether the trust can be established as being a sham. An allegation of sham against a Jersey trust goes to the validity of that trust and again, early consideration of Jersey's firewall legislation must be considered. An allegation of sham entails a finding that the parties to the trust dishonestly intended to present the trust as genuine.
- Whether the trust assets can be attributable to the settlor/beneficiary in another way, e.g. whether the way the powers and beneficial interests in the trust are arranged is such that the settlor/beneficiary has *de facto* control of the assets and has rights that are, in substance, equivalent to ownership e.g. *Pugachev* ([2017] EWHC 2426 (Ch)). The Jersey courts have never had to rule upon the analysis employed by Birrs J in the case of *Pugachev*. Whether the firewall would protect a Jersey trust from such an analysis remains an open question.

Financial disclosure

The financial disclosure obligations of a spouse in divorce proceedings filed in Jersey relating to their trust interests on a worldwide basis would be as follows:

- Each party to divorce proceedings must, following the preliminary directions hearing, file and serve an affidavit of means containing full particulars of all property, income and expenses of each party. This includes any interest either spouse has under a trust, located anywhere in the world, whether that interest is vested or contingent.

- The disclosing spouse is obliged to state the estimated value of their interest under the trust and state when, if ever, that interest is likely to be realisable. An interest under a discretionary trust must be disclosed. If a spouse believes that the interest may never be realisable or has (in the present or future) no value, they must provide their reasons for that assertion.
- In order to engage the Royal Court's jurisdiction under Article 27 Matrimonial Causes (Jersey) Law 1949 (the power of the court to vary a nuptial settlement), the particulars given about a settlement should include (or can be asked about in any subsequent questionnaire that follows receipt of the affidavit of means) the basis upon which the settlement was established and the circumstances by which it is said to have 'nuptial quality'.

The financial disclosure obligations of a trustee in divorce proceedings filed in Jersey where the trust is governed by Jersey law are as follows:
- Whether the divorce proceedings are commenced in Jersey or whether they are commenced outside of Jersey, unless the trustee submits to the jurisdiction of the divorcing court and is made the subject of an order for disclosure about the trust, there is no obligation of financial disclosure concerning the trust that is imposed upon the trustee simply because a beneficiary is going through a divorce.
- There is no standard way in which a beneficiary's interest can be structured under a Jersey trust. A beneficiary may have a fixed interest or can be an object of the trustee's discretion to apply income or capital in their favour, as is the case with a discretionary trust. It may be a mixture of the two.
- Whether or not the trustee submits to the jurisdiction of the divorcing court, when divorce proceedings are in prospect and one or both of the divorcing spouses is a beneficiary of the trust, the trustee should seek Jersey advice on whether it wishes to exercise its discretion to provide financial information concerning the trust and the beneficiaries' interest under it. The trustee's discretion to provide information and disclosure about a trust is independent of the divorce proceedings.
- A focused disclosure exercise of relevant information about a trust may, in the right circumstances, serve to head off what might otherwise be a credible threat to the trust and its assets posed by divorce proceedings. The trustee will need to make a decision (which it may also seek to have 'blessed' by the Jersey court) whether to provide financial information at all and, if so, what information, to whom, under what conditions (e.g. a confidentiality ring). This will always be fact specific exercise.

The financial disclosure obligations of a trustee in divorce proceedings filed in a foreign jurisdiction where the trust is governed by Jersey law would be as follows:
- A Jersey trustee has no obligation to provide disclosure about the trust or a beneficiary's interest under it simply because a beneficiary requests the trustee to provide disclosure. The trustee retains an independent discretion concerning whether, and if so what, to disclose to a beneficiary upon request.

- The tension that exists in answering any request for disclosure of information by beneficiaries is a balance of a number of factors: maintaining the confidence of the beneficiaries that the trustee is accountable; the trustee's duty of confidentiality to and between beneficiaries as a whole; the trustee's duty to preserve the trust fund from potential attack by a hostile party; and, lastly, the value the trustee may ascribe to maintaining a 'safe space' in which it is free to exercise its discretion and decision making without constant interference from beneficiaries.
- Jersey law has long recognised that the disclosure of trust information and documents is subject to an overriding judicial discretion and not hard-and-fast rules as to the beneficiaries' unassailable right or entitlement to documents or information. This discretion forms part of the court's overriding supervisory jurisdiction in relation to trusts and enables the court to intervene, where necessary, to protect the trust from an attempt by beneficiaries to obtain information that may be contrary to the interests of the beneficial class as a whole. (The leading Jersey case on the disclosure of trust information by trustees is *Rabaiotti* 1989 Settlement [2000 JLR 173]2); the approach adopted was later endorsed by the Judicial Committee of the Privy Council in the leading English decision of *Schmidt v. Rosewood Trust Ltd* [2003] UKPC 26, affirmed in Jersey by Re *Internine Trust* [2004 JLR 325].)
- The leading Jersey case law governing the principles applicable to the disclosure of information and documents to beneficiaries by trustees predates the current formulation of Article 29 Trusts (Jersey) Law 1984. In 2018 Article 29 was replaced in its entirety by a provision which better articulates the position that had been reached in the case law prior to its enactment.
- Article 29 now expressly provides that a beneficiary's *prima facie* entitlement to request any document which relates to or forms part of the accounts of the trust is subject to contrary provision in the trust instrument itself. A blanket prohibition in the trust instrument on the beneficiaries' access to accounts and information is very likely to be held to be ineffective.
- The key issue is whether restrictions in the trust itself on what may be disclosed encroach upon the overarching supervisory jurisdiction of the court.

Efficacy of foreign orders for disclosure

The order of a foreign court made directly against a Jersey trustee to provide disclosure about a Jersey trust is not enforceable against the trustee in Jersey. That is not to say such an order does not have effect in the jurisdiction in which it is made and a Jersey trustee that has any exposure to the jurisdiction of the matrimonial court may regard themselves as being bound by such an order regardless of whether the order is directly enforceable in Jersey.

A Jersey trustee caught between its duties of maintaining the confidentiality of the trust and a foreign order requiring disclosure will often seek the protection of the Royal Court for directions as to what it should do. The Royal Court may direct the trustee as to what disclosure and information it should provide in compliance with a foreign order for disclosure. A trustee who acts in accordance with such a direction cannot later be sued by the beneficiaries for breach of trust or confidence.

Letters of request

The principal means by which an order for disclosure against a Jersey trustee by a foreign court is given domestic effect in Jersey is by way of letters rogatory, or letters of request.

Part 2 of the Service of Process and Taking of Evidence (Jersey) Law 1960 provides for the taking of evidence in Jersey in proceedings held outside the island (referred to as 'the requesting court'). The Royal Court has a wide discretion to make such provision as it deems appropriate. This usually involves the production and transmission of documents from Jersey to the requesting court or for evidence to be taken in Jersey and that evidence to be transmitted and admitted in the foreign proceedings. Practitioners wishing to issue a letter of request to Jersey should contact local Jersey lawyers for advice as to the form and content of a letter of request which must satisfy a number of requirements. A letter of request that is too widely drawn, or strays into areas access to which is forbidden by the law of Jersey, may have those offending sections exercised or rejected (*Wadman v. Dick* (*n 224*)).

Financial orders

Obligations of a spouse beneficiary of a trust governed by Jersey law who is a party in divorce proceedings in which they have been ordered personally to pay income and/or capital to their spouse

A beneficiary that is ordered to pay income or capital to their spouse on the basis of a finding (or an assumption) by a matrimonial court that they can satisfy such an order by requesting a distribution from the trustee is in an invidious position.

In the absence of a power in the terms of the trust itself that is capable of overriding the powers of the trustees; a discretionary beneficiary of a Jersey trust generally has no power to force the trustees to make a distribution to them.

Even if a trustee was agreeable to making a distribution to a beneficiary to help satisfy a matrimonial award, a trustee may regard it as an abuse of its powers of distribution (and leave them open to an accusation of having acted in breach of trust) to make a distribution to a beneficiary knowing that in doing so the distribution will, in fact, end up in the hands of the beneficiary's spouse (who may not themselves be a beneficiary). Depending on the size of the award, the trustee may come under pressure from other beneficiaries not to make a distribution if that would diminish the overall size of the fund. The trustee may well wish to seek the protection of the Jersey court by seeking directions as to how it should proceed.

Recent Jersey authority *Kea Investments Ltd v. Watson* [2021] JRC 009 has confirmed that it is not possible for a judgment creditor, such as a spouse with an unsatisfied matrimonial award, to obtain execution against the interest of a discretionary beneficiary under a Jersey trust.

A matrimonial court may have reached the conclusion that a Jersey trust is a financial resource because of a lack of candour about the true nature of the spouses' interest and the court makes an adverse inference against them. Such a finding may also arise simply from a lack of relevant information, absent any issue of lack of candour. Disclosure about the trust and what the trustees are likely to do in response to a request from a beneficiary is therefore likely to be crucial to running (or defending) a case based on a Jersey trust being a financial resource available to a spouse in any case where that point is not expressly conceded.

To treat an interest in a discretionary trust as an asset for distribution in proceedings for a financial remedy, the court must conclude that the trustees "would be likely to advance the capital [in the trust to the spouse] immediately or in the foreseeable future" (see *Charman v. Charman* (No 2) [2007] EWCA Civ 503). The objective is to establish what the trustees are likely to do.

In English law it has been held to be wrong to put undue pressure on trustees to act in a certain way by making an award against a spouse in the expectation that the trustees will have little option other to assist the beneficiary meet their obligations. (*A v. A and St George's Trustees Ltd* [2007] EWHC 99, Munby J). The distinction between determining what the trustees will do and this sort of 'judicious encouragement' to do something is almost inevitably blurred.

While it may have the effect of putting pressure on the way a Jersey trustee would ordinarily go about its duties, judicious encouragement is not a direct interference with the way a Jersey trust operates and is not something that engages the firewall legislation. The firewall is in place to protect the trust from the external interference of a foreign court, it does not protect beneficiaries from having orders made against them that they cannot satisfy without the trustee's assistance.

Obligations of trustees of trusts governed by Jersey law with regard to court orders made in divorce proceedings filed in Jersey and requiring payment of income and/or capital

The Royal Court's jurisdiction to make an order varying the terms of a nuptial settlement is narrower than exists under section 24(1)(c) Matrimonial Causes Act 1973. The Royal Court's jurisdiction will only be engaged where the settlement has the necessary nuptial quality as "between the parties to the marriage", i.e. it must confer benefits upon its beneficiaries *qua* husband or *qua* wife.

Unless the trust falls within the scope of Article 27 Matrimonial Causes (Jersey) Law 1949, the Royal Court has no power to direct the trustees to exercise their direction in a particular way in favour of one spouse or another to satisfy a matrimonial order.

Where an order is made against a beneficiary as a form of judicious encouragement to the trustee, in the expectation that the beneficiary will be able to satisfy the order by asking for and being granted a distribution from the trust – answer is as in the above section.

Obligations of trustees of trusts governed by Jersey law with regard to orders made in divorce proceedings filed in a foreign jurisdiction requiring payment of income and/or capital

Any party to foreign matrimonial proceedings seeking to enforce or have effect given to a foreign judgment in Jersey that concerns a trust governed by Jersey law should be aware of the terms and effect of Article 9 of the Trusts

(Jersey) Law 1984 well in advance of any final order. The practical effect of the so-called 'firewall' is that in respect of a Jersey trust (Article 9 applies only to Jersey law trust) the Royal Court is forbidden from enforcing or otherwise give effect to any order of a foreign court on an issue falling within Article 9(1) which are:

- the validity or interpretation of a trust (the question of whether a Jersey trust is a sham is a question going to the validity of the trust);
- the validity or effect of any transfer or other disposition of property to a trust;
- the capacity of a settlor;
- the administration of the trust, whether the administration be conducted in Jersey or elsewhere, including questions as to the powers, obligations, liabilities and rights of trustees and their appointment or removal;
- the existence and extent of powers, conferred or retained, including powers of variation or revocation of the trust and powers of appointment and the validity of any exercise of such powers;
- the exercise or purported exercise by a foreign court of any statutory or non-statutory power to vary the terms of a trust (such as section 24 Matrimonial Causes Act 1973, or section 1 Variation of Trusts Act 1958); or
- the nature and extent of any beneficial rights or interests in the property;

unless the foreign court has applied principles of Jersey law in determining its judgment on that issue.

The purpose of Article 9 is to protect Jersey trusts from interference, variation or attack by foreign courts. This was a particular concern with regard to foreign court orders in the context of matrimonial proceedings, which purported to vary Jersey law trusts (for example: section 24(1)(c) Matrimonial Causes Act 1973; *Charalambous v. Charalambous* [2004] EWCA Civ 1030; *Minwalla v. Minwalla* [2004] EWHC 2823 (Fam) (declaring a Jersey trust to be a sham).

The firewall applies regardless of whether the trustee has engaged with or submitted to the jurisdiction of the foreign matrimonial court. The Royal Court does not have any jurisdiction simply to order a trustee of a Jersey discretionary to make a distribution from a Jersey trust to satisfy a foreign order for variation of the trust or to satisfy a lump-sum order.

However, Article 9 does not prevent the court giving effect to a letter of request sent to it from a foreign court for information or disclosure of documents, even where the information that is sought for foreign proceedings pursuant to the letter of request is information that the court could be expected to refuse disclosure of were the application made to it, sitting in its supervisory capacity (*J v. K and Ors* [2016] JRC110).

Prior to the enactment of the current version of Article 9, the Royal Court regularly gave effect to orders of foreign courts that had the effect of varying Jersey trusts. Article 9 was first amended in 2006 with the enactment of the Trusts (Amendment No 4) (Jersey) Law 2006. Those provisions are considered in many of the reported decisions concerning the recognition and enforcement of orders against Jersey trusts made in foreign matrimonial proceedings. In doing so it has expressed the view that it regarded it an exorbitant assumption of jurisdiction for a foreign court to seek to pronounce, on the basis of its own law, upon whether a Jersey trust was a sham which the Royal Court would be very reluctant to give effect to or enforce. The Royal Court has also expressed a desire that English courts, particularly the Family Division of the English High Court, exercise restraint and refrain from using their statutory jurisdiction to vary Jersey trusts under the Matrimonial Causes Act 1973 and ride roughshod over the distinct supervisory jurisdiction of the Royal Court to give appropriate directions to the trustee, which, in many cases, invariably replicated the effect of an English order for variation (*In the Matter of the B Trust* (n 6)).

Jersey law has no equivalent jurisdiction to that conferred by section 24(1)(c) of the Matrimonial Causes Act 1973. The Family Division of the Royal Court possesses a more limited statutory jurisdiction to vary a nuptial settlement under Article 27 of the Matrimonial Causes (Jersey) Law 1949. See *J v. M* [2002 JLR 330] for an understanding of postnuptial settlements in Jersey law, which is narrower (and so are the Court's powers) than the meaning of that phrase and scope of the jurisdiction to vary a settlement under the Matrimonial Causes Act 1973, section 24(1)(c).

It follows that there is no obvious Jersey law counterpart that could be applied by a foreign court so as to make the variation compliant with Article 9(1), nor an obvious reason why it would do so.

The respective functions of the foreign matrimonial court and Royal Court are different in the context of matrimonial disputes concerning a Jersey trust. The foreign court is concerned to do justice and achieve a fair allocation of assets between the spouses before it. In the exercise of that jurisdiction, the foreign court is not generally concerned to consider the other beneficiaries of the trust. The Royal Court, by contrast, is likely to be sitting its supervisory jurisdiction over the trust when the trustee returns to it for directions as to what it should do pursuant to the foreign matrimonial order. The primary consideration of the Royal Court will be to approve decisions that are in the interests of all the beneficiaries as a class, which may include one or both of the spouses (*In the Matter of the B Trust* [2006 JLR 532]).

The question then arises whether the Royal Court can recognise or give substantive effect to a foreign order purporting to vary a Jersey trust? It had been thought that the previous incarnation of Article 9, as the court identified in *In the Matter of the B Trust* [2006 JLR 532] did not exclude the possibility that the court may, as a matter of judicial comity, give effect to an order of a foreign court varying a Jersey trust. The leading reported decision on the previous version of Article 9 (*In the Matter of the IMK Family Trust*) suggests that the answer was yes (at least in so far as the foreign order effects a variation to a Jersey trust and not an alteration).

In *IMK Trust* it was held that, notwithstanding the prohibition on enforcement of a foreign order under Article 9(4), where the foreign order merely varied the trusts, the Royal Court could achieve the objectives of the foreign order, having regard to the interests of the beneficiaries as a class, under its discretionary supervisory jurisdiction. The giving of directions in this way was not said to amount to the enforcement of the foreign judgment for the purposes of Article 9(4). Conversely, a foreign order that amounted to an alteration could not be recognised or given effect to by the Royal Court as the court does not have an unfettered power to rewrite the terms of a trust outside of its statutory jurisdiction in Article 47 (*In The Matter of the IMK Family Trust* at [65]–[68], [78] and [80]; *Compass Trustees v. McBarnett & Ors* at [18]: 'the court cannot do what the trustees cannot do'). In giving effect to a foreign order varying a trust, the Royal Court was not exercising its jurisdiction under Jersey law to vary but is actually giving directions to the trustee pursuant to Article 51 of the Trusts (Jersey) Law 1984 concerning the administration of the trust.

However, the Article 9(4) considered by the court in IMK Trust has since been amended to prohibit the Royal Court enforcing or giving effect to the order of a foreign court that is inconsistent with Article 9. The court does not retain an overarching residual power to give effect to judgments on the basis of comity in the teeth of the statute. The Royal Court now has no power to enforce or otherwise give effect to a foreign order purporting to vary a Jersey trust that falls foul of the firewall.

Since Article 9 was extended to preclude the Royal Court giving effect to any judgment not in compliance with its terms, it is no longer even possible for the Royal Court to direct the trustees, acting within the powers that they have, in a way that would give substantial effect to such a judgment (*In The Matter of the R Trust* [2015] JRC267A). The prohibition on the Royal Court giving effect to a foreign judgment that falls foul of Article 9 is not expressed to be limited in any way.

The Efficacy of the Firewall

The practical efficacy of the firewall very much depends upon the location of the assets and of the trustee. Article 9 operates most effectively where the trustees and the trust assets are located within the territorial jurisdiction of the Royal Court. Where the trust assets are located outside of Jersey and so beyond the jurisdiction of the Royal Court to protect them the efficacy of Article 9 is likely to questionable, particularly if the assets are immovable or otherwise subject to the territorial jurisdiction of the matrimonial court. Where assets are at risk, the trustee is likely to need to apply to the Royal Court for directions: first, as to whether it should submit the jurisdiction of the foreign court and, secondly, whether (if it has power to do so) it should give effect to the foreign order.

Relevance of the trustee's decision to submit to the jurisdiction of a foreign court

It has been suggested that it will not generally be in the interests of the beneficiaries (as a class) for the trustee to submit to the jurisdiction of a foreign court in matrimonial proceedings in which one or both of the spouses are beneficiaries under the trust (*In the Matter of the H Trust* (n 6)). To do so would, on orthodox conflict of laws principles, confer a jurisdiction on the foreign court to act to the detriment of the beneficiaries who are not before it. Not submitting to the jurisdiction of the foreign court will, at the very least, preserve the trustee's freedom of action when a foreign order is sought to be enforced, at which point it is likely the trustee will once again seek the court's direction.

Under the current version of Article 9, submission to the jurisdiction of the foreign court is no longer the touchstone for the enforcement of the foreign decision in Jersey for judgments falling within its scope. Instead, the key question in respect of foreign judgments falling with the scope of Article 9 is whether the foreign court has applied Jersey law in its determination irrespective of whether the trustee has submitted. Of course, where the foreign order does satisfy the requirements of Article 9, the trustee, having voluntarily submitted to the jurisdiction of the foreign court, will not be able to seek to argue that the order should not subsequently be given effect to in Jersey.

Notwithstanding the foreign court's jurisdiction is no longer the central issue in respect of judgments falling within Article 9, the decision whether to submit to the jurisdiction is likely to be a momentous decision for which the trustee is usually well advised to obtain the direction of the Royal Court (*In re S Settlement* 2001 JLR N [37]).

The presence of trust assets within the jurisdiction of the foreign court is likely to be the most significant factor in the trustee's decision whether or not to submit to its jurisdiction because without submission to the jurisdiction, the trustee cannot practically defend those assets from enforcement in accordance with its duties (*In re A & B Trusts* [2007 JLR 444]).

Whether it does or does not submit to the jurisdiction of the foreign court it has been recognised that the trustee should provide the foreign court (whether directly by its own submission or via such of the beneficiaries that do submit if the trustee does not itself submit) with the fullest financial information concerning the trust to ensure any determination or settlement is based upon the true position and not supposition (*In the Matter of the H Trust*).

Another factor is whether or not the trustee's decision not to submit to the foreign court's jurisdiction is likely to leave the trustee open to criticism and even a breach of trust claim by the beneficiaries if the trust comes to be a varied by the foreign court to the prejudice of the beneficiaries who are not party to the matrimonial proceedings (*C.I. Law Trustees Limited v. Minwalla & Ors*).

The issue in the trustee's application for directions is not that the trustee needs a direction from the court as to whether it can satisfy the foreign judgment from the trust assets (the court has no jurisdiction to give that sort of direction if the foreign judgment has been reached contrary to Article 9(4)). The object of such an application is instead to enable the trustee to seek the Court's protection from the possibility of a breach of trust action being brought against it from disgruntled beneficiaries as a result of the trustee having effectively lost trust assets in the event of enforcement being taken against them in the foreign jurisdiction.

While Article 9 does not permit the court to direct the trustee to give effect to a variation so as to give effect to a foreign judgment, the Royal Court retains jurisdiction to bless a trustee's own decision to give effect to a foreign judgment. The approval of a momentous decision already taken by the trustees themselves is not an order enforcing or giving effect to a foreign judgment (*Otto Poon* [2011] JRC 167; [2014] JRC 254A). When deciding whether or not to bless a momentous decision, the court is not exercising its own discretion but is instead making a declaration that the trustee's proposed exercise of the power is lawful and reasonable. The consideration is whether the decision falls within the range of decisions that a reasonable trustee, properly exercising its power, is entitled to make.

There has yet to be a decision as to what a trustee should do where a foreign court has made a variation order, there are assets that are vulnerable to enforcement within the jurisdiction of the foreign court, but the trustee has no power (unlike in IMK) to give effect to the foreign order and so cannot seek the court's blessing of its own decision to give effect to the foreign judgment.

Enforcement

The Royal Court only has jurisdiction to sanction for contempt of its own orders (typically by way of fine, committal to prison or the sequestration of assets). The Royal Court will not directly enforce an order of a foreign court for contempt for non-compliance against a Jersey resident who is the subject of a foreign order.

To engage the Royal Court's jurisdiction to grant a sanction for non-compliance requires taking a step by which the Royal Court itself makes an order which would then have to be disobeyed in order to engage the Royal Court's jurisdiction to grant a sanction for contempt.

In the context of the disclosure of information, the Royal Court's jurisdiction would be engaged where it is asked to grant a freezing injunction with ancillary orders for disclosure in support of foreign matrimonial proceedings. The disobedience of that order would amount to a contempt of court, punishable by fine, committal or the sequestration of assets. Likewise, where the Royal Court receives a letter of request from a foreign court for the disclosure of relevant documents and information, the mechanism by which that is given effect in Jersey is by way of order from the Royal Court. Non-compliance is ultimately punishable by imprisonment, fine or the sequestration of assets.

Where compliance with a foreign order for capital or maintenance is sought in Jersey, for the Royal Court to give effect to such an order requires that the foreign order be recognised by the Royal Court and given effect to in Jersey. That is achieved either by way of formal registration (only available for judgments from certain jurisdictions) or by means of recognition at common law. Once that process is complete, it will have the effect of making the foreign order an order of the Royal Court. Disobedience of which will be punishable by committal to prison.

Jersey, somewhat unusually, also still has a procedure to commit a person to prison for debt (an *Actes à Peine de Prison*). Interim orders, usually taken out on an *ex parte* basis and under time constraints, may make provision for a person to be arrested and held in custody until such time as he produces security for the claim which is being made. Another case is where an interim order is made against a husband where there are arrears of maintenance and the husband is an expatriate (as in *Dick v. Dick*). The court may also make final orders for the arrest of a debtor pending satisfaction of the debt. These orders are almost invariably made in circumstances where the debtor, although enjoying a very high standing of living, has very few, if any, assets in his own name, probably because the assets are held by companies which may in turn be owned by discretionary trusts.

In the Dick case, the ECHR held that while a draconian interim measure may well cause considerable inconvenience, in the context of the Jersey proceedings as a whole, there was no unfairness that infringed Article 6.

2. PRENUPTIAL AND POSTNUPTIAL AGREEMENTS

A prenuptial agreement is a legal agreement made between two individuals before their marriage has taken place. A postnuptial agreement is made after the marriage. Whether pre- or postnuptial, the purpose of such an agreement is usually to set out how the couple wish their assets, income and earnings should be divided between them if they later separate or divorce.

A pre- or postnuptial agreement is not the same thing as a pre- or postnuptial settlement. This is a form of trust that is made in contemplation of marriage and benefits one or both parties to a marriage (*J v. M* 2002 JLR 330). The Royal Court has a limited jurisdiction to vary a nuptial settlement in some circumstances to make financial provision for the parties to the marriage or their children. Whether a trust is a nuptial settlement is often complicated and technical and requires specialist advice.

Jersey's traditional outlook had been that an agreement entered into before or after marriage to regulate affairs on future separation or divorce would not be upheld as it was contrary to public policy. The issue of prenuptial agreements has received limited consideration by the Jersey Court. Nuptial agreements are not binding in Jersey.

The Royal Court has considered the leading English case of *Radmacher v. Granatino* [2010] UKSC 42 in *L v. M* [2017] JRC 062A, finding that a prenuptial agreement is a factor to be considered as part of 'all the circumstances of the case', but the parties could not oust the overarching jurisdiction of the court by means of such an agreement. In this case reliance on the prenuptial agreement failed because the parties' needs and circumstances dictated a different outcome. The most that can be said is that the Royal Court may hold that a nuptial agreement should be given decisive weight. However, this will depend on the circumstances of the case and the terms of the agreement. In *G v. H* [2018] JRC111 the Royal Court again rehearsed the legal principles set out in *Radmacher* and other leading English cases. While it is likely that these factors would be considered by the Royal Court were the matter ever to come up, a detailed analysis of the circumstances in which the Jersey court would be prepared (or not) to uphold a pre- or postnuptial agreement has not yet reached the court and the law in Jersey waits to be clarified. Those factors are:

- Whether the parties have freely entered into it, with competent legal advice and with a full appreciation of its implications.
- Whether the agreement might be vitiated by duress or freely entered into.
- Whether there has been a material lack of information or disclosure before entering into the agreement.
- Whether and to what extent the agreement provides the needs of the parties.
- Whether and to what extent the agreement provides for the needs of any children of the family.
- Whether the agreement and its terms are fair in all the circumstances.

International issues often arise in cases involving nuptial agreements. That is especially so in Jersey, which, as an international finance centre, is familiar with divorces where one or both parties have an 'international lifestyle' where assets are spread across the world in all manner of trust and corporate structures.

There is no Jersey authority on the question of whether it makes a difference if a pre- or postnuptial agreement must be governed by Jersey law to be given effect in Jersey matrimonial proceedings. The answer is likely to be that it makes no difference. The determinative factors that are likely to impact whether the agreement is given effect to or not are those listed above.

In *Radmacher*, the Supreme Court said that an English court will normally apply English law when exercising its jurisdiction to make an order for financial remedy under the Matrimonial Causes Act 1973, irrespective of the domicile of the parties or any foreign connection. The position in Jersey is likely to be the same.

Procedural requirements

The existence of a pre- or postnuptial agreement, its terms and the basis upon which it was entered into, are factors to which the court is bound to have regard under Article 29 Matrimonial Causes (Jersey) Law 1949, as part of 'the conduct of the parties to the marriage insofar as it may be inequitable to disregard it and to their actual and potential financial circumstances.'

Spouse's financial claims

A pre- or postnuptial agreement can be entered into by spouses in respect of any part of the matrimonial 'pot' of assets, including assets not forming part of either spouses personal or joint estate (which would include assets held subject to a discretionary trust). It is not uncommon to see nuptial agreements that attempt to ring-fence trusts from the scope of matrimonial claims.

Children's financial claims

A pre- or postnuptial agreement can make provision for financial claims regarding a child of the family (whether living at the time of the agreement or who are planned). If a nuptial agreement fails to do so, or fails to do so adequately that is a factor that will weigh heavily with the court in deciding whether or not to give effect to the agreement.

3. THE MEDIA AND DIVORCE/FAMILY LAW PROCEEDINGS

The general practice in Jersey is that matrimonial and children proceedings are held in private (Royal Court practice direction RC 20/11). The information that can be published in respect of divorce cases is limited to the names, addresses and occupations of the divorcing parties and any witnesses, a concise statement of particulars, submissions and decisions on points of law and any judgment.

All children cases are held in private and nothing can be published which identifies or is likely to identify a child.

Members of the press do not have access to the Family division of the Royal Court. They do, however, have access to the published law reports, which are usually anonymised when they refer to children (and are increasingly subject to anonymity in any family matter).

It not usually the practice of the Royal Court to anonymise the names of professional trustees who may have become parties to divorce proceedings.

Reporting restrictions

Reporting restrictions will apply automatically to all matrimonial and children proceedings commenced in the Royal Court, which are, by default, held in private.

The mechanism by which the media may make applications to report on proceedings and having access to documents used in the proceedings is by way of an application to intervene and for access to be given to the court file, the pleadings and the affidavit evidence. The court's accession to such request is extremely rare and is likely to be hedged with a number of restrictions (e.g. the identity of a minor or facts that would enable the identification of that child will not be permitted).

AUTHOR BIOGRAPHIES

James Sheedy

James is Partner and qualified English Barrister and Jersey Advocate with a busy litigation practice focusing on trust and private wealth disputes. He is the author of Jersey's leading trust disputes text 'Litigating Trust Disputes in Jersey Law, Procedure and Remedies'. James advises and represents both beneficiaries and trustees in breach of trust claims; asset tracing/recovery against trusts and trustees; claims for secondary liability against accessories; disputes concerning trust administration; applications to court for directions, variation and rectification of trusts; disputes about disclosure; the appointment and removal of trustees; and disputes about the exercise of powers.

He advises on jurisdictional disputes and the enforcement of foreign judgments against trustees and beneficiaries. James also advises on a broad range of contentious and commercial and company law disputes.

Professional Memberships in include Contentious Trust Association (ConTrA); Association of Contentious Trust & Estate Practitioners (ACTAPS); The Chancery Bar Association; and Trust Law Working Committee of Jersey Finance.

Simon Thomas

Simon is Partner and qualified English Barrister and Jersey Advocate. Simon has over 25 years practical courtroom experience. He undertakes work which spans a number of diverse areas of law, including; contentious trusts litigation, commercial litigation, family & matrimonial law as well as employment law and public law. He is also skilled in the handling of cases with an international aspect, including; asset tracing and international legal assistance.

LIECHTENSTEIN

Johannes Gasser & Bernhard Motal
Gasser Partner

INTRODUCTION

24,000 corporations, foundations and trusts are currently under management in Liechtenstein, a significant number when compared with the principality's population of roughly 38,000. With 10,000 foundations, the civil law "alter ego" of the common law trust is still the most frequent asset protection structure in use.

Corporate laws date back to 1926, when Liechtenstein was the first jurisdiction in continental Europe to introduce the concept of an Anglo-Saxon trust. Liechtenstein's legal and fiduciary practice has employed these legal instruments with in-depth experience and expertise for nearly 100 years.

Liechtenstein is a civil law jurisdiction and, sandwiched between Switzerland and Austria in the heart of the Alps, often borrows both statutory and case law professionals for roughly 120 trust companies from these two neighbouring jurisdictions, including many esteemed members of the judiciary. Courts and regulatory authorities are known to work efficiently: they have the resources and know-how to facilitate swift registration and licensing, as well as confidentially resolve complex, often international disputes involving significant wealth.

Due to its asset protection strengths, Liechtenstein's foundations and trusts have often been considered ideal for protecting private wealth from the onslaught of creditors. This may include claims in family disputes, including divorce proceedings.

1. DIVORCE AND TRUSTS

The concept of trusts is recognized in Liechtenstein. In fact, Liechtenstein was the first country in continental Europe to recognize trusts by implementing them into positive law in Art. 897 to 932 Persons and Companies Act (*Personen- und Gesellschaftsrecht*) as early as 1926, i.e., nearly 100 years ago.

When a divorce is filed in Liechtenstein, if there is no agreement between spouses regarding the financial consequences of their divorce, the court must assess the maintenance and determine the division of assets in accordance with the principles of Art. 67 *et seq.* Marriage Act (*Ehegesetz*).

When assessing a maintenance claim, the spouse's income and assets, among other things, are taken into account (cf. Art. 68 (2) (e) Marriage Act). As a special asset, a trust could possibly be considered in the following cases:

- One of the spouses is the settlor and has, within the two years preceding the filing of an action for annulment of marriage, petition or action for divorce or separation, or, if the marital community has been dissolved prior to the filing of the action, at the earliest two years preceding such dissolution, reduced marital property or marital savings by initial or subsequent dedication of property to the trust property in a manner that is inconsistent with the spouses' living arrangements during the marital community (cf. Art. 84 [1] Marriage Act).
- One of the spouses is the settlor and has reserved a right of revocation.
- One of the spouses is a beneficiary of the trust, thus distributions from the trust are relevant for the maintenance assessment and the apportionment decision.

In the context of division proceedings, only division assets are considered, which includes any increase in assets achieved by the spouses during the marriage up to the dissolution of the domestic partnership which is not covered by exceptions specified in the law (Art. 74 Marriage Act). Pursuant to Art. 75 (1) (a) Marriage Act, assets which a spouse has brought into the marriage, acquired by reason of death or which a third party has transferred to them via a donation (*Schenkung*) shall not be included in the assets to be divided. Therefore, in many cases trusts may not be assessed in division proceedings. The division is made on an equitable basis (Art. 78 lit a Marriage Act).

If a divorce is filed in a foreign jurisdiction, the provisions of the Marriage Act already outlined above will not apply. Generally, it is not possible to seize the assets of a trust in Liechtenstein on the basis of a foreign court decision regarding a divorce, since foreign court decisions are generally not enforceable in Liechtenstein and enforcement agreements exist only with Austria and Switzerland. The situation may be different if the trust assets of a Liechtenstein trust are located abroad, because in this case the court(s) of the country in which the assets are located may have (sole) jurisdiction. Further, in Liechtenstein one can initiate the so-called *Rechtsöffnungsverfahren*, which is a kind of fast-track procedure in which foreign judgments are considered a suitable basis for a Liechtenstein enforceable title (*Rechtsöffnungstitel*).

1.1 Financial disclosure

In Liechtenstein divorce proceedings, generally, regarding both trust assets and other assets, spouses have an interest in the determination of mutual assets for the purposes of division proceedings and the assessment of maintenance. Although the law does not expressly grant a right to information and accounting in non-contentious proceedings (*Ausserstreitverfahren*), such a right is provided by Art. XV Introductory Act to the Code of Civil Procedure and the Jurisdiction Act (*Einführungsgesetz zur Zivilprozessordnung und der Jurisdiktionsnorm*) for civil procedures and applied analogously in non-contentious proceedings. The prerequisites are that the requesting spouse is able to provide information about any concealed or hidden assets and to certify a corresponding suspicion of asset concealment. Since, from the perspective of execution law, this information disclosure is a so-called non-substitutable act (*unvertretbare Handlung*), i.e., one that cannot be performed by third parties, it can only be executed with fines or imprisonment. The party may also be placed under oath, whereby a false statement constitutes a criminal offense under section 288 (2) Criminal Code (*Strafgesetzbuch*). Also, regardless of whether the party is under oath or not, an intentional false statement may constitute a fraudulent act within the meaning of section 146 Criminal Code. However, there are no instruments similar to contempt of court orders in Liechtenstein civil procedure law.

In cases where there are Liechtenstein divorce proceedings and Liechtenstein trusts, pursuant to Art. 923 (2) Persons and Companies Act, the trustee must render accounts and provide information to the auditor or, subsidiarily, to the settlor or, again subsidiarily, to the fixed interest beneficiaries, insofar as their rights are affected. Hence, members of a class of discretionary beneficiaries are not considered to have such rights to information. Moreover, professional trustees are subject to the duty of confidentiality (cf. Art. 21 Trustee Act [*Treuhändergesetz*]) and may be, in case of violation, subject to criminal prosecution.

Where the trust is not governed by Liechtenstein law, but by foreign law, such obligations are primarily governed by that foreign law. However, any trustee based in Liechtenstein will still be held to the general principle of confidentiality, and in cases of doubt, the trustee will need to seek advice or directions from the foreign court that has jurisdiction over the trust.

In cases where there are foreign divorce proceedings and Liechtenstein trusts, if a production order is addressed to a non-litigant based in Liechtenstein, the person making the request incurs criminal liability under Liechtenstein State Protection law, especially if coercive measures are used if the recipient refuses to comply with the order. If a Liechtenstein person is a party to such proceedings, cooperation with a foreign court order is legitimate as long as there are no sanctions and the party is free to dispose of the relevant documents. The deciding factor for triggering the blocking order in the Liechtenstein State Protection Act (*Staatsschutzgesetz*) is the amount of coercion used when making the request. The two highest courts of Liechtenstein, the Supreme Court and the Constitutional Court, took rather different views in a series of recent decisions. Ultimately, the Constitutional Court criticized the other courts involved for, according to the Constitutional Court, wrongly assuming that a beneficiary who was ordered by the Irish Supreme Court in divorce proceedings to request information from a Liechtenstein foundation was under no threat of being sanctioned. The Constitutional Court stressed that anyone complying with such contempt of court orders may be at serious risk of criminal prosecution in Liechtenstein, although it allowed the Irish beneficiary to receive the requested information on their beneficial interest from the foundation, as there was already a final judgment ordering the information to be divulged. Parties to foreign proceedings ordered to request information from a Liechtenstein party thus need to be very careful when considering, as the Constitutional Court ruled, the "sensitivity" of such cases and requests (see Constitutional Court docket no. 2021/064, LES 2022, 25). Where contempt of court orders carrying the threat of sanctions are imposed on such parties, it is unlikely that Liechtenstein courts will grant the application.

1.2 Financial orders

The creditors of a spouse beneficiary in a case involving Liechtenstein divorce proceedings may assert a claim against trust property by way of initiating execution or bankruptcy proceedings, but, according to Art. 914 (2) Persons and Companies Act, only insofar as the beneficiary has claims against trust property. However, the settlor may stipulate in the trust deed (*Treuhandurkunde*) that a beneficial interest which has been acquired against no consideration may not be withdrawn from a beneficiary by way of execution or bankruptcy proceedings. In this case, the creditors of the beneficiary have no claim against the trust property. The same applies to decisions made by courts in foreign jurisdictions, if these decisions are to be recognized in Liechtenstein law.

Trust assets are absolutely excluded from the trustee's creditors' executive access pursuant to Art. 915 Persons and Companies Act. However, creditors of the beneficiary can assert their claims against trust assets according to Art. 914 (2) Persons and Companies Act, but only if the beneficiary has a legal claim against trust assets, i.e., is not a mere discretionary beneficiary (*Ermessensbegünstigter*), or if the beneficiary is settlor and has reserved powers of revocation. The trustee is liable for obligations at the expense of trust assets only if it is not proven that the third party did not rely on a more extensive liability. As mentioned above, if trust assets are situated abroad, the court(s) of the country in which the assets are located may have jurisdiction.

The same applies if the basis for the payment obligation is a divorce ruling recognized in Liechtenstein. However, if a spouse is a discretionary beneficiary (*Ermessensbegünstigter*) of a Liechtenstein trust and lives abroad, they need not fear a lawsuit in Liechtenstein: according to a decision by the Liechtenstein Supreme Court there is no domestic jurisdiction in this case and a lawsuit would be dismissed. However, this does not apply in cases where there are grounds for suspicion of damage to creditors.

1.3 Enforcement

As mentioned above, Liechtenstein (procedural) law does not provide for instruments like contempt of court orders. If a payment obligation is not met, it can be enforced in execution proceedings pursuant to the Code of Execution (*Exekutionsordnung*). This may result in the seizure and liquidation of assets, but not imprisonment of the obligated party. However, obligated parties may, as a last resort, be subject to fines or imprisonment if disclosure cannot be provided by third parties.

2. PRENUPTIAL AND POSTNUPTIAL AGREEMENTS (PNAS)

Liechtenstein law regarding the monetary consequences of divorce is regulated in the Marriage Act (Art. 73 to 89a *leg cit*). The assets to be divided under matrimonial property law are described in Art. 74 Marriage Act as "any increase achieved by spouses during marriage up to the dissolution of the domestic partnership which is not covered by the exceptions listed in this Act". Thus, in Liechtenstein, in principle, any asset that cannot be subsumed under one of the explicitly listed exceptions pursuant to the Marriage Act is subject to division under matrimonial property law.

Liechtenstein matrimonial property law provides for a deviation from this prescribed division order in very few exceptions. Pursuant to Art. 89a (1) Marriage Act, the division of matrimonial property may not be waived by contract in advance.

According to Art. 89a (2) Marriage Act, however, it is permissible for spouses to contractually agree (before or during the marriage) that companies or shares in companies are to be excluded from the division under matrimonial property law, provided that these are not mere investments. However, pursuant to Art. 89a (3) Marriage Act, agreements regarding the modification of the division of the total increase in assets in the meaning of Art. 74 Marriage Act can only ever be made with legal effect in (timely) connection with impending marriage annulment, divorce or separation proceedings.

If foreign parties agreed on a prenuptial or postnuptial agreement, Liechtenstein courts will generally enforce and uphold such agreements, provided that there was a valid choice of foreign law and that there are no public policy issues that would suggest the PNA, or parts thereof, to be disproportionate or discriminatory. In such cases Liechtenstein courts are likely not to enforce the PNA and consider it invalid.

2.1 Procedural requirements

According to Art. 89a (4) Marriage Act, agreements pursuant to Art. 89a (2) Marriage Act must be in writing and the signatures must be notarized in order to be legally binding. Agreements within the meaning of Art. 89a (3) Marriage Act, however, require court approval.

2.2 Spouse's financial claims

Agreements modifying the division of marital property system are not limited to the election of a matrimonial property regime but, as outlined above, are only permitted in very specific circumstances.

2.3 Children's financial claims

Pursuant to Art. 89g Marriage Act, in the event of a divorce the provisions of the General Civil Code (*Allgemeines Bürgerliches Gesetzbuch*) govern the settlement of (financial) child support.

However, in any case, no agreement between the parents may be made that is detrimental to the child. This would be deemed an inadmissible and ineffective so-called contract to the detriment of third parties (*Vertrag zulasten Dritter*). Nevertheless, parents going through a divorce could, for example, contractually agree to divide child support among themselves or to pay higher child support than provided for by the law. Under no circumstances, however, may the amount of child support be reduced in such an agreement. In simple terms, all provisions in such agreements that are to the detriment of the child are invalid.

3. THE MEDIA AND DIVORCE/FAMILY LAW PROCEEDINGS

Pursuant to Art. 140 (1) Non-Contentious Matters Act (*Ausserstreitgesetz*), oral hearings in all non-contentious matrimonial and child-related matters are not public. Only if all parties to the proceedings agree may the public be allowed to attend oral hearings by court order, provided that no circumstances of private and/or family life are to be discussed and provided it is compatible with the welfare of the person (child) in care. Thus, the best interests of the fostered person (child) are always the centre of focus. In the case of contentious divorce proceedings the hearing and the pronouncement of the judgement are not public either, pursuant to § 522 Code of Civil Procedure (*Zivilprozessordnung*).

Third parties who are not parties to the proceedings (members of the media) may only physically participate in oral hearings in matrimonial and child-related matters if the hearing is public, which, however, is only possible in exceptional cases pursuant to Art. 140 (1) Non-Contentious Matters Act. Further, remote attendance by video link is not possible even if the oral hearings in family law matters are made public, since Liechtenstein civil procedural law does not provide for public attendance to oral hearings via remote media of communication.

In principle, it is not possible for the media to gain access to court documents or publish information from them. Pursuant to § 219 (2) Code of Civil Procedure, third parties may only gain access to court documents with the consent of the parties to the proceedings and, moreover, only insofar as this does not conflict with the overriding legitimate interests of another party or overriding public interests. In the absence of such consent, third parties may gain access to court documents only if a legal interest in the inspection of court documents is shown to be credible. Members of the media, however, have no legal interest in gaining access to court documents.

Even if an oral hearing should be made public in individual cases, cameras and recording devices are nevertheless not permitted, since Liechtenstein civil procedural law prohibits the production of recordings during public hearings in general, i.e. not only in matrimonial and/or child-related matters.

3.1 Reporting restrictions

Liechtenstein civil procedural law does not provide for a formal application to restrict reporting by the media. However, such an application is unnecessary: as described above, public presence at oral hearings in family law matters and the inspection of court documents by third parties is only possible if all parties to the proceedings give their respective consent.

AUTHOR BIOGRAPHIES

Johannes Gasser

Johannes Gasser is Senior Partner of GASSER PARTNER Attorneys at law, formerly Batliner Gasser, one of the leading law firms in Liechtenstein and a Chambers Global top tier firm, which was established in 1954. Johannes Gasser is ranked by Chambers Global as a "leading individual" in Liechtenstein. He is admitted to the Liechtenstein and Austrian Bar and specializes in advising UHNWI in setting up, administrating and challenging and defending Liechtenstein foundations and trusts in international litigation and arbitration. Johannes is a frequent speaker at the Liechtenstein University and University of Innsbruck (Austria) on foundation and trust law issues and legal expert witness in UK and other courts on Liechtenstein law. He is a member (Trust Estate Practitioner/TEP) of the Society of Trust and Estate Practitioners (STEP), an academician of The International Academy of Estate and Trust Law (IAETL) and an International Fellow of the American College of Trust and Estate Counsel (ACTEC).

Bernhard Motal

Bernhard Motal is a Counsel of GASSER PARTNER Attorneys at law. He is admitted to the Liechtenstein bar and also took the bar exam in Austria. Bernhard advises international clients and specialises in the areas of foundation and trust law, asset protection, estate planning and international private law. He regularly represents clients in domestic and international trust and foundation disputes (arbitration and litigation) and inheritance and divorce proceedings. He is author of numerous books and articles in renowned legal journals. In 2017, he won the prestigious Kathrein Privatbank Foundation Award in Austria with his doctoral thesis "Fundamental Questions of Liechtenstein Persons- and Corporate Law". Before joining Gasser Partner Attorneys at law in 2019, Bernhard worked in the corporate law department of a renowned Austrian law firm, as research and teaching assistant at the Department of Civil law at University of Vienna and as research Assistant at the Austrian Supreme Court, where he has acquired outstanding expertise in his fields of work.

NEW ZEALAND

Anita Chan KC & Richard Reeve
Princes Chambers

INTRODUCTION

This chapter concerns relationship property, trusts and asset protection in the legal jurisdiction of Aotearoa New Zealand.

This area of law is governed by statute, namely the Property (Relationships) Act 1976 (PRA) and the Family Proceedings Act 1980 (FPA).

The PRA is the primary legislation governing division of property following separation. It applies to married couples, couples in a civil union and couples who have been living in a *de facto* relationship. The general scheme of the Act is that following separation all personally owned assets are classified as either relationship property or separate property. Relationship property is divided equally while all separate property assets remain the separate property of their owner. The Act provides limited remedies for parties whose rights under the Act have been defeated by the transfer of personally owned assets to a trust.

The FPA provides the courts with a broad discretion to provide a separated party with a remedy in respect of nuptial trusts after the marriage or civil union has been dissolved. Such remedy is not available to *de facto* couples.

1. DIVORCE AND TRUSTS

Trusts have long been part of New Zealand law, with the High Court exercising jurisdiction over trusts both in an inherent capacity and pursuant (now) to the Trusts Act 2019. As stated, the courts have limited jurisdiction to address trust issues after relationship breakdown.

In New Zealand, divorce (known as a dissolution of marriage) is distinct from separation. To apply, an applicant must swear evidence that the parties have been living apart for at least two years. Conversely, the end of a *de facto* relationship is standardly deemed to take place on the date of separation, though a *de facto* relationship must typically have lasted at least three years before statute-based relief in respect of relationship property is available.

When a party applies for a relationship property division where there are trust interests, the court has limited power under sections 44 and 44C of the PRA either to order that compensation be paid to one party from the trust, or to claw back assets into the relationship property pool. However, the court does not have power under the PRA to divide trust property *per se*.

Another Act, the FPA, contains a discretionary provision – section 182 – empowering the court to enquire into property settled into trust provided that the trust is nuptial in nature. The FPA however does not apply to *de facto* relationships. Section 182 does not mandate an automatic equal division of trust property. Rather, the court has discretion to make orders with reference to the application of the whole or any part of trust property, or vary the terms of a settlement, either for the benefit of children of the marriage or civil union or of one or both parties.

In recent decades, the courts have shown themselves willing to declare constructive trusts in relation to certain trust property even though that property seems to fall outside the relationship property pool. Such scenarios are however heavily fact-dependent.

Where a divorce has been filed overseas, any order for division of relationship property will only have force if the parties consent to it having application in

New Zealand, or if rules of recognition apply. If the parties do not agree and there are no applicable rules of recognition, new proceedings will need to be filed.

Financial disclosure

In proceedings, a party's financial disclosure obligations standardly entail the production of affidavits of assets and liabilities. Discovery is a feature of most civil proceedings (and a court may order pre-proceedings discovery or discovery from a third party).

For completeness, section 44B of the PRA permits the court to make an order requiring a party to disclose specified information relating to the disposition of relationship property to a trust. This can be on the application of either party or on the court's own initiative.

If a trust is nuptial, the trustee will be obliged to disclose some, but not all, information associated with the trust and its property. That information may include core trust documents and information concerning the nature of trust property. However, confidential documents – such as deeds of distribution, memoranda of wishes or even sensitive commercial information – may remain outside the scope of discovery. Whether information is confidential must be assessed on a case-by-case basis.

The core criterion for discovery is relevance to the proceeding. While the court of Appeal has in the past held that ordering an unequal division of relationship property on the basis of immovable offshore assets would constitute an unjust interference with another country's sovereignty (where those immovable assets were located), there is no simple answer to the question of what must be disclosed.

Offshore trust interests may or may not have relevance to a proceeding subject to the applicability of the New Zealand jurisdiction (see section 7 PRA; section 4 FPA), any rules of recognition, and whether the parties consent to the New Zealand jurisdiction in respect of those interests.

There is no obligation in New Zealand law for a trustee to disclose information for the purpose of divorce proceedings filed overseas, unless those proceedings have been transferred into the New Zealand jurisdiction, or the parties have consented to New Zealand law applying.

However, if one party to the proceedings has any standing under the New Zealand trust, they may be able to obtain the information sought pursuant to Part 4 of the Trusts Act 2019. Importantly, these statutory provisions apply irrespective of whether proceedings have been issued.

Financial orders

The starting point is that a spouse/partner beneficiary cannot be ordered to make either income or capital payments from trust property which they do not control. Only a trustee can be ordered to pay from trust property.

Both sections 44 and 44C of the PRA contain mechanisms addressing the alienation of property into trust to defeat another party's claims. Section 44 permits a court to set such a disposition aside. However, relief may be denied if the property or interest was received in good faith and the recipient has so altered their position in reliance on the settlement that it would be inequitable to grant relief. Section 44C(2) grants the court power to make compensatory orders, including:

- an order requiring one spouse or partner to pay to the other spouse or partner a sum of money, whether out of relationship property or separate property;
- an order requiring one spouse or partner to transfer to the other spouse or partner any property, whether the property is relationship property or separate property;
- an order requiring the trustees of the trust to pay to one spouse or partner the whole or part of the income of the trust, either for a specified period or until a specified amount has been paid.

It should be noted that "separate property" under section 10 of the PRA includes "property that a spouse or partner acquires from a third person−[...] because the spouse or partner is a beneficiary under a trust settled by a third person". Separate property is <u>not</u> relationship property, and cannot be treated in a relationship property division except in accordance with selected provisions such as section 44C(2)(a) and (b) above (along with others elsewhere in the Act).

Importantly, the remedies under section 44C(2) are only available once the court is satisfied there has been an alienation of relationship property into trust with the consequence of defeating the claims or rights of one party. Moreover, the remedies in section 44(C)(2) are only available when the clawback mechanisms in section 44 are unavailable.

An order under section 44C(2)(c) is an order of last resort:

"The court must not make an order under subsection (2)(c) if−

(a) an order under subsection(2)(a) or (b) would compensate the spouse or partner; or

(b) a third person has in good faith altered that person's position−

   (i) in reliance on the ability of the trustees to distribute the income of the trust in terms of the instrument creating the trust; and

   (ii) in such a way that it would be unjust to make the order."

Orders under section 44C(2) are enforceable pursuant to either the court's procedural rules, the Contempt of Court Act 2019 or section 121 of the District Court Act 2016 (which grants the High Court overarching jurisdiction to enforce orders made by the lower courts where those courts lack the ability to do so themselves).

An order from a foreign jurisdiction requiring a trust beneficiary to pay income or capital to a spouse or partner will only be enforceable in New Zealand if the parties consent to that order having application, or if rules of recognition apply. Otherwise, fresh proceedings may be required.

As discussed, the court retains jurisdiction to compel the trustees of a nuptial trust in limited circumstances to make an income-based distribution to a beneficiary's spouse or partner (PRA section 44C(2)(c)), or order payment from the trust capital to a beneficiary's spouse or partner (or their children) (FPA section 182(1)), or vary the terms of the trust settlement in favour of a beneficiary's spouse or partner (or their children) (also FPA section 182(1)).

While a beneficiary cannot be obliged to pay compensation from trust property which they do not control, the Supreme Court has identified in *Clayton v. Clayton* [2016] 1 NZLR 551 that certain residual powers in a nuptial discretionary trust can themselves constitute an interest. If such powers were acquired during the relationship, they are properly classified as relationship property even though the discretionary beneficiary may appear to have "only a hope" to receiving the trust property itself (i.e., no vested interest).

Regarding the Vaughan Road Property Trust, the *Clayton* court asked itself, what was the correct value of the residual powers? Its conclusion was that, in that case, the powers were "equal to the value of the net assets of the VRPT". The implication was that, even if neither the capital nor the income of the trust could be accessed by the other party, the value of the trust itself nevertheless needed to be factored into the relationship property pool.

Where trustees are subject to a court order, they must comply or face the penalties arising from contempt of court. While the court may not have jurisdiction to address offshore property directly, it retains power to compel a person to undertake certain actions or face a personal sanction. Thus, even though the New Zealand Court may have limited or no power over offshore assets, the Contempt of Court Act 2019 grants it various powers of enforcement over people situated in New Zealand including imprisonment, fines, sentences of community work and, in the case of the High Court, sequestration orders.

No order made offshore will be enforceable either against a party personally or against the assets of a trust (whether or not the assets are located here) unless the order has been resealed or the court has assumed jurisdiction because of the parties' agreement.

Enforcement

As a matter of general law, no person shall be arrested or imprisoned for default in payment unless the default triggers the exceptions in section 3(2) of the Imprisonment for Debt Limitation Act 1908. Those exceptions include:

- default in payment of a penalty or sum in the nature of a penalty other than a penalty in respect of any contract;
- default in payment of any sum recoverable before the District Court under the Summary Proceedings Act 1957 or otherwise than under the District Court Act 2016;
- default by a trustee or person acting in a fiduciary capacity, and ordered to pay by a court having jurisdiction in the matter any sum in his possession or control.

Section 16 of the Contempt of Court Act 2019 creates a general power of enforcement of certain orders or any undertaking given to the court if, on the faith of the undertaking, the court has sanctioned a particular course of action or inaction. However, this power remains subject to section 17 of that Act.

Section 17 states that section 16 only applies if the case in question falls into the exceptions in section 3(2) of the Imprisonment for Debt Limitation Act 1908 (see above) "or the order applies to money held by a person, trust, or entity other than the defaulter". Section 17 further provides that only the High Court may take action under section 16 to enforce a court order for recovery of land.

Under section 16(4)(a)(i), a court may issue a warrant committing a person to imprisonment not exceeding 6 months. However, it must not do so unless satisfied that other methods of enforcement have been considered and are inappropriate or have been unsuccessful (section 16(3)(a)). If so satisfied, the court must make a finding under section 16(3)(b) as to whether it is proved beyond reasonable doubt that:

- the court order or undertaking being enforced has been made in clear and unambiguous terms and is clearly binding on the person; and
- the person had knowledge or proper notice of the terms of the court order or undertaking being enforced; and
- the person has, without reasonable excuse, knowingly failed to comply with the court order or undertaking being enforced.

Any enforcement order does not operate to extinguish the liability of the person to comply with the court order or undertaking.

2. PRENUPTIAL AND POSTNUPTIAL AGREEMENTS (PNAS)

PNAs are enforceable in New Zealand under Part 6 of the PRA.

PNAs executed in an offshore jurisdiction may be enforceable here provided certain formal requirements are satisfied.

Section 2 of the PRA specifies, for Part 6 of that Act, that the "lawyer" witnessing a party's signature (and certifying that that party has had the effect and implications of the agreement explained to them) must be:

- in the case of a document signed in a Commonwealth country outside New Zealand, […] a lawyer (as defined in section 6 of the Lawyers and Conveyancers Act 2006), or a solicitor entitled to practise in that country, or a notary public;
- in the case of a document signed in a country that is not a Commonwealth country, […] a lawyer (as defined in section 6 of the Lawyers and Conveyancers Act 2006), or a notary public.

Section 6 of the Lawyers and Conveyancers Act 2006 defines "lawyer" to mean "a person who holds a current practising certificate as a barrister or as a barrister and solicitor."

Procedural requirements

Section 21F of the PRA states that a PNA is void unless it complies with four statutory requirements. First, the agreement must be in writing and signed by both parties. Second, each party must have independent legal advice before signing. Third, the signature of each party must be witnessed by a lawyer. And fourth, the lawyer who witnesses the signature must certify that, before that party signed the agreement, the lawyer explained the effect and implications of the agreement.

Importantly, those four statutory requirements do not limit or affect any enactment or rule of law or equity that makes a contract void, voidable, or unenforceable on any other ground (section 21G). Moreover, the court has jurisdiction under section 21H to give effect to an agreement, whether wholly or in part or for any particular purpose, even though it may not comply with section 21F. The court's statutory jurisdiction also extends to setting a PNA aside if it is satisfied that giving effect to the agreement would cause serious injustice (section 21J), though there are certain mandatory considerations.

Spouse's financial claims
Section 21A(1) of the PRA permits the parties to make any agreement they think fit with respect to the status, ownership, and division of property owned by either or both of them. "Property" is expansively defined in the PRA to include real property, personal property, any estate or interest in any real property or personal property, any debt or any thing in action, or any other right or interest. As such, a PNA may address trust property even though that property is not *per se* relationship property.

Children's financial claims
PNAs can deal with financial arrangements regarding children notwithstanding that the Inland Revenue has jurisdiction over child support pursuant the Child Support Act 1991, and can override a PNA if its terms do not meet default minimum standards.

3. THE MEDIA AND DIVORCE/FAMILY LAW PROCEEDINGS
Subject to any judicial direction to the contrary, accredited news media reporters can attend both the Family Court and the High Court, and report on proceedings. However, a judge has authority to direct reporters to leave the courtroom (or not attend remotely) where sensitive matters or vulnerable persons (especially children) are involved. A judge must grant permission before a reporter can film, take photographs or make sound recordings in court.

Section 11B(1) of the Family Court Act 1980 permits "any person" to publish a report of proceedings in the Family Court. Importantly, this is subject to subsection 3, which requires leave from the court to publish a report on proceedings that includes identifying information in respect of either a person under the age of 18 or a "vulnerable person" (as defined in section 11D). Subsection 3 does not apply to reports that are genuinely of a professional or technical nature and which do not include the names of any person under the age of 18, "vulnerable persons" or schools. Subsection 3 also does not apply to publication of purely statistical information.

Reporting restrictions
Any person can apply for reporting restrictions. However, the application's success will depend on whether the applicant can show that identifying information will arise in respect of a "vulnerable person" (as defined in section 11D of the Family Court Act 1980) or a person under the age of 18.

"Identifying information" is defined to include any name or particulars likely to lead to the identification of any of the following persons:

a) a party to the proceedings;
b) an applicant in the proceedings;
c) a person who is the subject of the proceedings;
d) a person who is related to, or associated with, a person referred to in paragraphs (a) to (c) or who is, or may be, in any other way concerned in the matter to which the proceedings relate (for example, a support person for a party).

For completeness, where proceedings have been initiated under the Oranga Tamariki Act 1989 (formerly known as the Children, Young Persons and Their Families Act 1989), "identifying information" also includes "the name or particulars likely to lead to the identification of any school that a person the subject of the proceedings is or was attending".

As stated above, any person – including reporters – may publish a report of Family Court proceedings, but leave is required where the report includes identifying information in respect of a person under the age of 18 or a "vulnerable person". The Ministry of Justice publishes an application for media to apply for permission from the judge to film, record or take photographs in court, which form must be filed within a specified timeframe.

AUTHOR BIOGRAPHIES

Anita Chan

Anita Chan KC is one of New Zealand's leading family lawyers. She was appointed to the rank of Queen's Counsel in 2014. Her practice is in complex property and child disputes. She is often briefed in cases involving farms, trusts, high-value assets, and complex asset structures, and cases involving international issues. Anita is a passionate advocate for children and is regularly appointed by the Court to act for children.

Anita is the Chair of the FairWay Resolution Ltd Board. She is a former Governor, Parliamentarian, Counsel and Vice-President of the International Academy of Family Lawyers (IAFL) and a former Chair of the New Zealand Law Society Family Law Section.

She is a proud graduate of the University of Otago.

Richard Reeve

Richard Reeve is a barrister sole at Princes Chambers in Dunedin. Richard has acted in a wide range of high-value and/or complex matters involving trusts and estates, relationship property and asset-planning arrangements. A graduate of the University of Otago, Richard also holds a Ph.D in the Humanities and is a well-known New Zealand poet as well as a lawyer.

SCOTLAND

Gillian Crandles & Zaynab Al Nasser
Turcan Connell

INTRODUCTION

The Scottish approach to financial provision on divorce is set out in the Family Law (Scotland) Act 1985, a detailed statutory framework with the primary aim of achieving fairness. Significantly, the legislation provides a clear definition of what falls to be divided between the parties, distinguishing between assets that were or were not acquired during the marriage through the efforts of the parties. The result, therefore, is a legal system which offers, as a starting point, a level of protection that is not available to spouses or civil partners separating in certain other jurisdictions.

Nevertheless, the protections are not comprehensive, and for various reasons spouses or civil partners may wish to take additional steps to ensure that their assets are not vulnerable to a claim in the event of marital breakdown. Similarly, where wealth has accumulated over generations, there may be concerns about the impact of a divorce on the interests of not just the separating spouse but their wider family.

In those circumstances, people often turn to asset protection solutions such as trusts or nuptial agreements, in the hope of reducing their exposure in the event of a future separation. Broadly speaking these will be respected by the Scottish courts who recognise the freedom of individuals to contract as they see fit, but they will also take a critical view of such arrangements where there is a question of fairness.

1. DIVORCE AND TRUSTS

Trusts have long been recognised in Scotland, governed by a succession of Acts over the course of the 1800s and consolidated in the Trusts (Scotland) Act 1921. They can offer flexibility and bespoke solutions for a variety of purposes including the protection of family wealth in the event of marital breakdown.

The regime governing divorce and financial provision in Scotland is contained within the Family Law (Scotland) Act 1985. The principles to be applied by the court in determining what orders for financial provision should be made (if any) are contained within section 9. The starting point is section 9(1)(a) which states that "the net value of the matrimonial property should be shared fairly between the parties to the marriage", with the same principle applying to partnership property in the case of civil partnerships.

Matrimonial or partnership property is defined by section 10(4) as all property belonging to the parties or either of them at the date of separation and which was acquired before the marriage for use as a family home or during the marriage but before the date of separation. There are exceptions for assets received by way of gift or inheritance from third parties.

The treatment by Scottish courts of trusts and trust assets in the context of a divorce will depend on whether they fall within the definition of section 10(4) – i.e. do they *belong to* one of the parties as at the date of separation? This will invariably require a consideration of the construction of the trust, the nature of the party's interest and the extent to which they have any control over what they receive from the trust.

In the case of a bare trust, for example, where the spouse/partner beneficiary has a defined interest, that will be clearly identifiable as property belonging to them. Discretionary trusts, on the other hand, where the distribution of capital or income is entirely within the control of the trustees, can reasonably be said not to fall within the definition of "property belonging to" the spouse/partner beneficiary.

In certain circumstances, however, the Scottish courts have been prepared to treat the assets of a discretionary trust as property belonging to the beneficiary in the context of an action for divorce. In the case of *AB v. CD* 2007 FamLR 53 the Lord Ordinary concluded that where the trust had been established by the husband for the purpose of protecting certain assets from creditors, and where there was evidence that the husband was directing the management of the trust assets and instructing payments from the trust, then the trust was simply being utilised by him as his "piggy bank".

Where a spouse/partner has transferred property to a trust which might otherwise have constituted matrimonial property at the date of separation, this could be treated by the court as an avoidance transaction, the effect of which is to defeat a claim for financial provision or aliment. Section 18 of the 1985 Act provides that the court may set aside or vary any transfer or transaction involving property effected by the other person not more than five years before the making of the claim. There is a time limit for the making of an application for an order under this section of one year from the date of disposal of the claim.

Section 18 also allows the court to interdict a person where such a transfer or transaction is anticipated. The use of interdict for these purposes is not limited to the spouse/beneficiary, and it is open to the party seeking such an order to join trustees as defenders (*M v. M* 2009 SLT 608 (OH); 2009 SLT 750 (IH)).

Although the capital value of a trust may be left out of account in the determination of matrimonial property and the appropriate division thereof between the parties, it remains open to the court to treat the income derived from a trust as a resource of the spouse/partner beneficiary for other purposes. These could include where the court is making an assessment of claims for spousal or child maintenance (known in Scotland as aliment), or simply when considering what resources are available from which an order for financial provision could be met.

Financial disclosure

Spouses/partners are expected to make full and frank disclosure of all of their assets for the purposes of identifying the matrimonial property available for division on divorce. This includes overseas assets and will include trust assets where they constitute property acquired during the marriage and belonging to one or both of the parties at the date of separation.

It is generally accepted in Scotland that beneficiaries have a right to certain information and that trustees of Scottish trusts, therefore, have a corresponding duty to provide that information. However, the law in this area is undeveloped in Scotland, with the main authority coming from Lord Clyde in *Nouillan v. Nouillan's Exrs* 1991 SLT 270: "trustees [are] bound to give a beneficiary full information about their administration and let [them] see the vouchers as well as the accounts". To the extent that such information is made available to a spouse/partner beneficiary and is in turn relevant to divorce proceedings, that information ought to be disclosed.

If there is a concern that certain assets have not been disclosed, the Scottish courts can be asked to order the disclosure of information through a Commission and Diligence procedure. Where the trustee of a trust in Scotland is considered to be a person in possession of the required information (known as a "haver"), they may be called upon to disclose any relevant documentation. If the trustee is of the view that the information is confidential, they may lodge the documents with the court in a sealed envelope. The court will then determine whether or not those documents should be disclosed in the context of the divorce proceedings.

If the trust assets, and therefore the trustee havers, are situated abroad, it may be necessary to proceed by way of letters of request, in terms of the 1970 Hague Convention on the Taking of Evidence Abroad in Civil or Commercial Matters. In those circumstances, however, the obligations of disclosure of a trustee of an offshore trust will be governed by the law pertaining to that trust, and advice should be taken in the relevant jurisdiction.

Trustees can be joined as defenders to divorce proceedings, and in certain circumstances the trustees may wish to become involved with a view to protecting the interests of the beneficiaries of the trust. By becoming a party to the action, however, the trustee will have certain disclosure obligations to the court, and they will require to balance these with their confidentiality obligations. In the case of an offshore trust, the trustees may simply refuse to submit to the jurisdiction of the Scottish court.

Where divorce proceedings have been filed in a foreign jurisdiction which is a signatory to the 1970 Hague Convention, and disclosure is required in relation to trust assets held in Scotland, letters of request may be received by the Court of Session with a view to obtaining evidence that is intended for judicial proceedings. The trustee will require to consider their position carefully, and may wish to take seek direction from the court as to how they should respond in light of their duty to the beneficiaries of the trust.

Financial orders

Section 8 of the 1985 Act sets out the various financial orders that can be sought in an action for divorce in Scotland. These include payment of a capital sum, property transfer, pension share and, in very specific circumstances, a limited form of maintenance known as periodical allowance. In making such an order, section 8(2) requires the court to have regard to certain principles as set out in section 9 of the Act and, importantly, the resources of the parties.

Resources are defined by the 1985 Act as "present and foreseeable resources", and could therefore reasonably be said to include access to trust property, although there is a shortage of Scottish authority on the point. Where the court has determined that the spouse/partner beneficiary has an identifiable and accessible interest in trust property (such as in a bare trust) or where they are deemed to exercise significant control over the management of the trust assets (as in *AB v. CD* above), it seems likely that such a resource would fall within the court's assessment. Similarly, where a beneficiary has a life interest which has always made, and will continue to make, regular income payments, it can legitimately be said to form part of the spouse/partner beneficiary's resources.

Any financial order made by the court in an action of divorce must be complied with by the spouse/partner against whom it has been granted. Failure to do so can result in enforcement action being taken against the defaulting spouse/partner. Enforcement can take a number of forms, referred to collectively in Scotland as diligence, including bank arrestment, earnings arrestment, attachment of property or money and inhibition orders.

The rules for recognition and enforcement of a foreign judgment in Scotland vary according to the jurisdiction of the original judgment. Where a jurisdiction is not covered by a specific enactment, the foreign judgment must be enforced by raising an action for decree of conform in the Court of Session. Once a foreign judgment has been registered, it can be enforced in the same way as a domestic judgment.

Enforcement

Where decree has been granted but payment is not forthcoming, and enforcement action requires to be taken against assets held within a trust in respect of which the debtor is a beneficiary, arrestment will be the most appropriate form of diligence. This allows money or moveable property to be arrested in the hands of a third party, such as a trustee, who has an obligation to account to the debtor, such as a beneficiary. The effect is to freeze the property so that it cannot be transferred to the debtor without the consent of the creditor before the arrestment is resolved.

Where a beneficiary has an ascertainable entitlement to payment under the terms of the trust deed, and provided such payments are not alimentary in nature, the right is moveable and therefore arrestable. However, the right of the arrester is no greater than that of the debtor, and therefore where a trustee has the power to restrict or vary payment under a trust, they may exercise their power to defeat an arrestment (*Chambers' Trustees v. Smith* (1878) 3 App. Cas. 795).

2. PRENUPTIAL AND POSTNUPTIAL AGREEMENTS (PNAS)

The enforceability of PNAs in Scotland has yet to be fully tested before the courts. As a matter of course, however, the Scottish courts are reluctant to interfere with an agreement entered into between two adults of sound mind, and the widely held view is that a PNA will be upheld provided that it was fair and reasonable at the time it was entered into.

Foreign PNAs should be capable of enforcement in Scotland, and section 10(6) of the 1985 Act expressly provides that a court should have regard to the terms of any agreement between the parties when making its assessment of how matrimonial property should be divided.

Procedural requirements

The main challenge to the enforceability of a PNA is that it was not fair and reasonable at the time that it was entered into, and that is the basis on which a court will set aside an agreement, or part thereof, in terms of section 16 of the 1985 Act. The principles the court will consider are set out in the case of *Gillon v. Gillon* 1995 SLT 678, as follows:

- the agreement should be examined for both fairness and reasonableness;
- the court should examine the relevant circumstances leading up to and prevailing at the time of execution of the agreement, including the nature and quality of the legal advice given to either party;
- if there is evidence that advantage had been taken by one party of the other by reason of circumstances prevailing at the time of the negotiation, this might have a bearing on the court's determination of the issue;
- the court should not be unduly ready to overturn agreements validly entered into; and
- the fact that an agreement results in an unequal division of assets is not sufficient on its own to give rise to any inference of unfairness or unreasonableness.

Spouse's financial claims
The ordinary purpose of a PNA in Scotland is to ring-fence certain assets to protect them from a claim on separation or divorce. Specifically, PNAs can be utilised to extend the protections afforded by the relevant legislation to non-matrimonial property to any assets that are derived from such property during the marriage, and which would otherwise be treated as *prima facie* matrimonial property and therefore vulnerable to a claim on divorce.

It is also possible for PNAs to set out specific financial provision on divorce, in relation to both capital division and maintenance, although this is more unusual. The same requirements as set out above would apply, and provided each spouse/partner enters the agreement on an informed and voluntary basis, it is unlikely a court would interfere with the terms of such a PNA where it was fair and reasonable at the time it was entered into.

Children's financial claims
Whilst there is nothing to prevent a PNA from making provision for child maintenance, it is worth noting that the Child Support Act 1991 makes clear that either parent of a qualifying child is entitled to apply to the Child Maintenance Service for a maintenance calculation which would override such provision. The only restriction on such an application being made with respect to a child is in circumstances where the parties have entered into a maintenance agreement which has been in force for less than one year. Whilst this is a useful provision in the context of Separation Agreements, its application will clearly be limited in the case of PNAs.

3. THE MEDIA AND DIVORCE/FAMILY LAW PROCEEDINGS
Scottish courts have a long tradition of open justice and, other than in specific and limited circumstances, the media will be allowed to attend and report on court proceedings.

In general terms, where legal proceedings in Scotland are heard in public, they are capable of being reported provided such publication is contemporaneous and in good faith, failing which they are liable to be treated as being in contempt of court (Contempt of Court Act 1981). The court may, however, determine that it would be appropriate to postpone or restrict such publication, and there are specific statutory exclusions relating to family law and child cases.

Undefended and simplified divorce actions are dealt with in chambers, and therefore do not call in open court. The consequence is that such cases cannot be reported until decree of divorce has been granted, at which time the media would have access to the names of the parties and the date on which they were divorced.

The Judicial Proceedings (Regulation of Reports) Act 1926 provides that, in the case of actions of divorce or dissolution, the media may only publish:
- the names, addresses and occupations of the parties and witnesses;
- a concise statement of the orders sought and the defences;
- details of any legal issues arising and the view taken by the court; and
- the final judgment and any observations made by the judge.

Where proceedings involve a child aged 16 or under, the court may, in terms of section 46 of the Children and Young Persons (Scotland) Act 1937, make an order that the child or children must not be capable of being identified by any newspaper report. This would normally mean that any subsequent judgment will be anonymised.

No such order is required in respect of a child concerned in exclusion order proceedings by virtue of section 44 of the Children Scotland Act 1995, and likewise section 182 of the Children's Hearings (Scotland) Act 2011 makes provision for a child involved in a children's hearing or other proceedings under the Act – in both cases, the relevant sections simply provide that any publication that could identify such a child is prohibited. Similarly, adoption and permanence proceedings are heard and determined in private in accordance with section 109 of the Adoption and Children (Scotland) Act 2007, unless the court decides otherwise. Again, where a judgment is produced, this will ordinarily be anonymised so that the parties, and the child(ren), cannot be identified.

Unless specifically excluded by statute, members of the media may be permitted to attend proceedings that are closed to the public (*Sloan v. B* 1991 SC 412). They may utilise live text-based communications whilst within a courtroom, but they are nevertheless expected to adhere to the reporting restrictions noted above. Photography is not permitted within court buildings without prior judicial approval, and similarly electronic devices may not be used with the exception of solicitors who may use them for the purposes of proceedings only.

Reporting restrictions

Where the relevant reporting restrictions do not automatically apply by operation of statute (as set out above), parties may prevail upon the court's general discretion in terms of the Contempt of Court Act 1981, section 11 of which empowers the court to prohibit publication of a name or a matter in connection with the proceedings. Any such order must, however, be sent to any interested person, which will include the press, and must be published on the Scottish Courts & Tribunals website. This may have the unintended consequence of drawing their attention to an action that might have otherwise proceeded unnoticed.

Where a judge exercises their discretion to impose reporting restrictions, they must first make an interim order which specifies why they are making the order. They must thereafter allow any interested person the opportunity to make representations before making a final determination on the matter. Once an order has been made, it remains open to any person 'aggrieved' by such an order to apply for its revocation or variation.

There is also scope for the relaxation of reporting restrictions in relation to children's hearings and other proceedings under the Children's Hearings (Scotland) Act 2011 where to do so would be in the interests of justice.

AUTHOR BIOGRAPHIES

Gillian Crandles

Gillian Crandles is Managing Partner and Head of Divorce and Family at Turcan Connell. She is one of Scotland's leading divorce lawyers and is accredited as a specialist by the Law Society of Scotland. According to Chambers UK, Gillian "has a very big reputation and it is well-deserved". Dealing with complex, high-net-worth cases, she has extensive expertise in cases involving business valuations, partnerships, and farming, as well as disputes involving significant cohabitation claims. She has a particular interest in international cases including disputes involving children, and jurisdiction for financial claims. She is dual-qualified in Scotland, England and Wales, and is frequently instructed in cases with a cross-border element, particularly in relation to asset protection, prenuptial, and postnuptial agreements. Gillian has a keen interest in alternative dispute resolution, and is a qualified collaborative lawyer, family mediator and arbitrator. She is a member of the Family Law Association and Resolution, and a fellow of the International Academy of Family Lawyers (IAFL).

Degree type: M.A. (Hons) in Italian and English Literature and LL.B. from the University of Edinburgh. Year graduated: 1998

Zaynab Al Nasser

Zaynab Al Nasser is an Associate in the Divorce and Family Law Team at Turcan Connell. She has practised exclusively in the area of family law since 2014, advising on a range of areas including financial provision and child related matters. She has experience in dealing with complex, high net worth cases, including those with an international element such as competing jurisdictional claims and foreign assets. She advises clients in relation to asset protection, including pre and post nuptial agreements, as well as cohabitation agreements for unmarried couples. Zaynab is regularly instructed in relation to disputes involving children, including contact, residence and relocation. She is a member of the Scottish Family Law Association and a Lay Advisor to the Royal College of Physicians and Surgeons of Glasgow.

University: University of Leeds; BPP Law School; University of Glasgow

Degree type: BA (Joint Hons) in English Literature and TESOL; LL.B. (Hons) in English Law; LL.B. in Scots Law. Year graduated: 2008; 2009; 2011

SOUTH AFRICA

Zenobia du Toit

Miller Du Toit Cloete Inc.

INTRODUCTION

The question arises in matrimonial proceedings whether trust assets should be included or excluded for the purpose of determining a party's estate.

As a general rule, if a trust has been properly formed (i.e., is a valid trust and not a sham), then it is likely that none of the trust assets will form part of any divorce settlement or court order, and the assets will continue to be uninterruptedly held in trust (Walter D Geach Trust Law in South Africa (2017) at 440).

Broadly in the instance of a trust being a "sham" (a valid trust never came into being), or a court piercing the veneer of a trust (based on company law principles related to piercing the corporate veil) distinct remedies are available. On the basis of the so-called *Badenhorst* principle a court may make an order against a party based on the value of assets held in trust by a party with control after the trust. The *actio Pauliana*, where assets are fraudulently alienated, is also discussed.

1. DIVORCE AND TRUSTS

Trusts are recognized and regulated by the Trust Property Control Act 57 of 1988, and based on English and Roman Dutch rules, as developed by the courts. A legal relationship is created by agreement between the founder and the trustees. Ownership of trust assets vest in the trustees who exercise fiduciary duties for the benefit of beneficiaries. Assets exist separately from the founder, trustees and beneficiaries.

If a trust is valid, it is unlikely that the trust assets will form part of any divorce settlement where a divorce is filed in South Africa.

Trust property does not automatically form part of a party's estate in divorce proceedings. The courts regard a trust as a legitimate estate planning tool and have been reluctant to include such assets as part of a party's estate upon divorce. Whether the trust's veneer should be pierced and whether the trust was created to devalue the other party's claims, will depend on each case's circumstances, the trust's formation and its use.

In *P A F v. S C F* (788)/2020) [2022] ZASCA 101 the Judge noted:
- There is a distinct difference between a trust being the "alter ego" of a trustee and a trust being a "sham".
- If a trust is the so called "alter ego" of a trustee, it does not follow that the assets of such trust vest in the estate of the trustee.
- It must be found that the trust was a "sham", and created and administered fraudulently.

Van Zyl and Another NNO v. Kaye NO & Others 2014 (4) SA452 (WCC) (endorsed by the Supreme Court of Appeal) held "maladministration of an asset validly vested in a properly founded trust does not afford a legally cognisable basis that the trust does not exist, or that the asset no longer vests in the duly appointed trustees".

"Going behind the trust form...essentially represents the provision by a court of an equitable remedy...that lends itself to a flexible approach to fairly and justly address the consequences of an unconscionable abuse of the trust form in given circumstances. It is a remedy that will generally be given when the trust form is used in a dishonest or unconscionable manner to evade a liability, or avoid an obligation."

This is derived from common law and not from any general discretion a court may have. In the context of accrual determination on divorce, it "is not based on the authority of the Matrimonial Property Act 88 of 1984 (MPA) or in the exercise of a statutory discretion", but "on a factual inquiry that has revealed trust form abuse, upon which the piercing of the trust veneer follows".

In a sham trust the transaction will have no legal effect, and the ostensible founder will remain the owner of the trust assets and neither the trustee(s), nor the beneficiaries will acquire any rights with regard to these assets. The "trust assets" will be taken into account as assets in the spouse's personal estate.

Alter ego trusts, where a person exercises *de facto* control over trust property, only describes the nature of the control exercised, and does not equate (as a sham does) to a juridical basis for taking trust assets into account for the purposes of patrimonial claims (*REM v. VM* 2017).

The use of the trust form to evade an obligation, whether relating to accrual or maintenance, will generally be sufficient for the court to pierce the veneer of the trust to prevent unconscionable abuse of the *form* of the trust.

The *actio Pauliana* is a Roman law remedy applied in the context of fraud on creditors generally, where the debtor had impoverished himself to the detriment of his creditors, e.g. by alienations, incurring liabilities or allowing rights to lapse. The remedy is available where transfer of assets is made into trust by a spouse with the intention of defrauding a marriage partner or their potential matrimonial claims in an impending divorce action gratuitously or without proper consideration in fraud of the creditor.

A spouse who transfers property to a trust to defeat an accrual claim does so in fraud of the other spouse's contingent claim to share in the accrual, and a claim under the *actio Pauliana* may apply.

In *PAF v. SCF*, it was held that: "Spouses with accrual claims acquire a protectable contingent right against each other, which the law will protect in circumstances of irregularity and a lack of *bona fides*."

If there has been unconscionable abuse of the trust form to avoid an obligation, the court may pierce the veneer of the trust and deem certain trust assets to be a part of the spouse's personal estate.

In marriages concluded before 1984 (when the accrual system came into effect), in a trust over which the relevant spouse has *de facto* control of trust assets (such that may enable him/her to utilize the trust as an alter ego), the court is empowered to take such assets into account when calculating an equitable distribution on divorce, but not to actually distribute trust assets.

The South African court will have no jurisdiction over assets in a foreign jurisdiction. If the South African court has jurisdiction in a divorce, the domicile of the husband at date of the marriage determines the marriage regime applicable to the parties' marriage. In terms of section 7(9) of the Divorce Act, and the rules of South African private international law, the South African court has the same power as a competent court of the foreign state concerned to order that assets be transferred from one spouse to the other spouse. Disclosure may take into account the law of the foreign jurisdiction.

An argument exists that trusts are sacrosanct as separate entities and should be dealt with in terms of South African law.

1.1 Financial disclosure

In terms of Rule 35 of the Uniform Rules of Court, in the case of a divorce filed in South Africa, a party has to make discovery on oath of any and all documents in the action, which are, or have at any time, been in the possession or control of such party and relevant to the action, and to disclose where such documents are, if not in his possession. Further and better discovery may be requested. A formal request for further particulars with detailed questions for information (and not documents) may be submitted.

Relevance is decided by the court having regard to the issues and the pleadings in which disputes are delineated (*Swissborough Diamond Mines (Pty) Ltd v. Government of the Republic of South Africa 1999* (2) SA 297 (T) at 311A).

Disclosure is relevant to the type of marriage in South African law, as follows:

- **Marriage in community of property.** An undivided joint estate is formed and the parties' ability to contract independently is limited.
- **Marriage out of community of property prior to the commencement of the MPA in 1984.** A redistribution order (in terms of section 7(3) of the Divorce Act) as the court deems just and equitable may be granted.
- **Marriages out of community of property with PNA after 24 November 1984:**
  - The accrual regime. A party claims 50% of the difference between the accrual of the parties' respective estates (except for exclusions). It sometimes states that a party may not establish a trust without the other party's consent and may exclude loan accounts in and distributions from a trust.
  - Marriages out of community of property excluding the accrual regime. This regime excludes any kind of redistribution claims. The Constitutional Court in February 2023 will consider the possible incorporation of a discretionary redistribution claim.

Personal maintenance claims

Section 7(2) of the Divorce Act 70 of 1979 ("Divorce Act"), provides that a court must consider *inter alia* the parties' existing means, in exercising their discretion as to the existence and content of a personal maintenance claim. "Means" include a party's access to funds, from a trust.

Disclosure, relating to a trust entails, *inter alia*:

- Distributions, loan accounts, journal entries, relevant resolutions.
- If a trust has been joined to proceedings and faces a claim to pierce the veil or that dispositions to a trust be set aside then the historical trust resolutions, disposition of assets to the trust, financial and management statements, bank statements, journal entries, notes, tax returns, dividend policies, the trust deed, valuations of assets, etc, may be relevant.
- Documents regarding the trust's subsidiaries (which is debatable as to relevance). A new judgment has put relevance in issue in these instances.
- Documents required by expert accountants.

Where divorce proceedings are filed in South Africa, if a trustee is a party to proceedings and the trust is governed by South African law, the financial documents relevant to the disputes between the parties, on the pleadings, shall be discovered.

Subpoenas may be issued against trustees and the trust's subsidiaries and the relevance thereof may be challenged.

The South African court has no jurisdiction to order disclosure by trustees of an offshore trust unless the trustees are parties to the proceedings. Proceedings are launched in the jurisdiction where the trustees are, in terms of the laws of that jurisdiction. A South African law court may, on application, request a foreign court to interrogate the trustees in terms of a questionnaire.

1.2 Financial orders

In a case involving a South African trust and South African divorce proceedings, a maintenance order only lies against a spouse personally. However, the spouse's means and income, assets and liabilities and access to funds will be taken into account, such as historical access to funds from the trusts. A court will not make an order against the trustees for personal maintenance obligations or make a distribution to the other spouse, even if that spouse is a beneficiary. The trustees will exercise a fiduciary discretion, taking into account the other beneficiaries, which may be tested in court.

A spouse beneficiary, who has been ordered to pay either income or capital to their spouse by a court cannot be required to do so from an uncertain contingent future right to trust assets. The discretion to distribute trust benefits rests with the trustees and is not vested in the beneficiaries.

The spouse's credit loan account in the trust may be attached by warrant of execution.

Where divorce proceedings have been filed in a foreign jurisdiction and an order has been validly granted, that order will be implemented in South Africa.

In terms of section 13 of the Divorce Act, the validity of a divorce order granted in a court of a foreign country or territory shall be recognised by a court in South Africa, if, on the date on which the order was granted, either party to the marriage was domiciled in the country or territory concerned, whether according to South African law or according to the law of that country or territory, or was ordinarily resident in that country or territory or was a national of that country or territory and provided there were legitimate proceedings and/or a legitimate order had been issued.

Where court orders made in divorce proceedings filed in South Africa require payment of income and/or capital against trustees of trusts governed by the law of South Africa, if the trustees are party to the proceedings, the trustees are bound to the order. This is, however, highly unusual.

Beneficiaries do not have vested rights in a discretionary trust.

A spouse beneficiary does not have a vested right to trust benefits. The discretion to vest assets rests with the trustees. The trustees cannot be forced to make a distribution. The benefit has to be accepted by the beneficiary to accrue. A beneficiary can call up a loan account, depending on the terms thereof.

Where the trust assets are situated both inside and outside of South Africa, the South African court will only have jurisdiction over assets in its area and will apply South African law.

In a case involving a South African trust and foreign divorce proceedings, if there is no order against the trustees, the trustees have no obligations, except their fiduciary obligations in terms of the trust deed.

Where the court has determined that it is likely that the spouse beneficiaries will be able to obtain distributions from the trusts for the purposes of paying all or part of the divorce award the trustees would have no obligations to make distributions to the spouse beneficiary. Distributions would be at the discretion of the trustees exercising their fiduciary duties and applying the provisions of the trust deed.

A South African court would not have jurisdiction in regard to trust assets outside its area, but has jurisdiction over assets within South Africa. Should a valid order against trustees be registered in South Africa, the South African court will implement the order.

1.3 Enforcement

Should a party be in contempt of a court order, the court can order a term of imprisonment or a fine to be paid and make a costs order. The applicant has the onus to prove that the court order was granted, served or that the respondent had knowledge of the court order, and that the court order was not complied with. A presumption arises that the non-compliance is wilful and *mala fide*. The respondent has an evidentiary burden to show reasonable doubt and, failing which, contempt will be established. This form of civil contempt is a crime, and can be prosecuted. A committal could be ordered in both civil and criminal proceedings.

If financial disclosure is not complied with, provided a court is of the view such disclosure is relevant, and the trust is a party, the trustee may be compelled to reply, failing which the trustee may be in contempt.

2. PRENUPTIAL AND POSTNUPTIAL AGREEMENTS (PNAS)

PNAs are recognised and enforceable in South African law. Section 6 of the MPA deals with the requirements relating to PNAs and section 21 regulates the amendment of matrimonial property regimes postnuptially.

Section 87(2) of the Deeds Registries Act 47 of 1937 governs the formality requirements of PNAs executed outside SA. It is attested by a notary, or otherwise entered into in accordance with the law of its place of execution. It shall be registered in a deeds registry within 6 months after the date of execution. The PNA has to be notarially executed before the marriage.

If the PNA is a foreign agreement, provided that the PNA has been validly concluded in terms of the foreign jurisdiction, effect will be given to it.

The South African court shall have the same power as a competent court of the foreign state would have had in regard to the PNA.

2.1 Procedural requirements

A Notary executes a PNA.

The contract must be concluded before marriage and registered in the Deeds Office before or after marriage, if signed in South Africa within three months and outside SA within six months of signature.

Postnuptially, application may be made to the High Court for an order to amend the regime in terms of section 21 of the MPA, after which a PNA is concluded and registered.

A PNA executed in accordance with the forms required by the law of the place of execution, should be recognised as being formally valid and binding everywhere, (*ex parte Spinazze and Another NNO* 1985 (3) SA650(A)).

There are no legislative or judicial guidelines prescribing time for consultation, reflection, independent legal advice and/or financial disclosure. This is currently under discussion by the South African Law Reform Commission (SALRC).

As a general rule South African courts uphold the provisions of PNAs and do not have an overarching discretion to divide matrimonial assets on an equitable basis in conflict with the provisions of a PNA after 1 November 1984.

The widening of the South African court's equity discretion to override the provisions of PNAs, executed after 1 November 1984, is being considered by the SALRC generally and the Constitutional Court (limited to marriages by PNA excluding accrual sharing).

2.2 Spouse's financial claims

Waiver of personal maintenance is contrary to public policy (*ST v. VCT* 2018(5) SA479 SCA). PNAs are usually limited to the election of a matrimonial regime. Parties may agree in the PNC to exclude distributions they receive from a trust or loan accounts a party may have in existing trusts, from a sharing regime, and agree that assets will not be disposed of to a trust and/or a new trust formed without the parties as beneficiaries, or without their consent.

Trustees cannot be bound by the PNA and are not parties to the PNA.

2.3 Children's financial claims

The High Court is the upper guardian of children. Any financial claims relating to children cannot be fixed or capped in the PNA, would not be enforceable and contrary to public policy.

3. THE MEDIA AND DIVORCE/FAMILY LAW PROCEEDINGS

Subject to the authorisation granted by a court in exceptional circumstances, the publication of the identity of, and any information that may reveal the identity of, any party or child in any divorce proceedings before any court, is prohibited. Failure to comply with the order will amount to contempt of court.

The special privacy of children and the principle of open justice, as well as freedom of expression, which enables public scrutiny of the courts, will have to be balanced.

Section 28(2) of the Constitution precludes the media from publishing the names and further particulars of a minor child.

In practice, the media reports on family law matters unlawfully from time to time, if they are considered to be in the public interest. A member of the media cannot record the proceedings without making an application to court first.

Court documents are publicly available from the court registrar. The media physically attends court hearings (which are public), but may not record the proceedings, unless an application to court for a permit is made.

3.1 Reporting restrictions

A party may apply to have the court file sealed in limited circumstances, e.g. in the event of competing rights and the right to privacy or harm to a minor child. Proceedings relating to a minor are usually held *in camera*. Anonymous publication may have limited value for parties involved in a high profile case and may create further curiosity in the public arena. High profile cases may be classified as exceptional circumstances, but the factors for exceptional circumstances are undefined. A court would look at whether publication is in the interests of justice. The public may have an interest in the information, particularly the parties' identity.

The identities of the parties have been published internationally, on BBC and CNN, which renders the prohibition ineffective.

AUTHOR BIOGRAPHY

Zenobia du Toit

Zenobia du Toit is Director at Miller du Toit Cloete Inc ("MDT"), a firm in Cape Town, South Africa, specializing in all aspects of family law, related constitutional law issues, comparative law, international cases, Hague Conventions, high end financial disputes, trusts, ADR, PNAs, children's interests, LGBTQI issues, ART and with a keen interest in developing family law.

She has written numerous articles, participates regularly in panels, webinars and expert forums. She has *inter alia* co-edited a textbook Family Law in South Africa (2021), comments regularly on draft legislation and the SA Law Reform Commission issue papers. She is a member of the IBA Family Law Committee and a governor of the IAFL.